One Who Reads Is Always Booked

Reviews of Books Too Good to Miss

Donna DeLeo Bruno

One Who Reads Is Always Booked
Reviews of Books Too Good to Miss

By

Donna DeLeo Bruno

Visit our website at **www.StillwaterPress.com** for more information.

First Stillwater River Publications Edition

ISBN-10: 0-997-87789-8
ISBN-13: 978-0-997-87789-2

1 2 3 4 5 6 7 8 9 10
Written by Donna DeLeo Bruno
Published by Stillwater River Publications, Glocester, RI, USA.

Dedication

This work is dedicated to my three "guys."
FB: My captain, my buoy, my anchor, my chart
From the very first day that you captured my heart
MBB (DMD)
BAB, (VP)
And my two precious grandchildren
Aerin and Nicholas
I knew you in my heart before you were even born.

TABLE OF CONTENTS

HISTORICAL FICTION

NON-FICTION

GREAT BOOKS

OTHER OUTSTANDING READS

Introduction

Thomas Jefferson wrote in a letter to John Adams: "I could not live without books." And so this is true of me also. To say that I love books is an understatement. I have associated them with pleasure for as long as I can remember --when as a small child my mother would read to me my favorite *The Five Little Peppers and How They Grew.*

Later as a young girl -- *The Nancy Drew Mysteries* -- and later yet, when in junior high school and in my "medieval" stage, a very tiny and elderly librarian, Miss Jessie Molasky, introduced me to *The Count of Monte Cristo, The Three Musketeers, Ivanhoe,* etc. I anticipated with delight the hour on Friday afternoon when all ninth graders would sit in her presence in the library, where perched on a high stool this wizened, elfin creature would turn into a damsel in distress imprisoned in castle towers while a courageous, chivalric knight stormed the fortress to rescue and release her. I was an incurable romantic from the beginning. A master of dialects, foreign accents, and brogues, Ms. Molasky transported me vicariously to distant lands and earlier times. She was an inspirational influence on me. It was with this fondness for words and literature that I became a teacher at Barrington High School in Rhode Island where I remained for 35 happy and gratifying years. For me it was a vocation.

Nothing pleased me more than sharing my love of books, poetry, and drama with my students, acquainting them with Shakespeare's exquisite imagery, discussing the universality of his themes, analyzing the psychological rendering of his characters, appreciating the sheer beauty of his language. When a pupil would begin to "hear" this poetic "music," I felt successful in my endeavors. I do not exaggerate the satisfaction I derived from sharing what I loved best with them, for "Good teaching comes not from behind the desk, but from behind the heart."

Of course, there were encounters with reluctant learners. On the first day of school one September, a new student announced proudly that he had NEVER read an entire book from cover to cover, and I replied that perhaps he hadn't yet been introduced to a "really great" book. In addition, I challenged him to remember this statement at the end of the year in June, anticipating that when I guided him to something that resonated or "spoke" to him in some way, he would become a convert. I believed that it didn't matter so much WHAT they read, as long as they ENJOYED the experience and were motivated to seek out books independently.

Speaking of reluctant students, one day long after I had retired, a GE repairman appeared at my door to fix my oven. Upon entering the house, he smiled and greeted me with,

"You don't recognize me, do you?"

Picking up on his cue, I surmised that he must have been one of my thousands of former students.

I replied, "Don't tell me. Give me a bit of time."

While I sat at my kitchen table balancing my check-book, he began work on the oven and started to reminisce. He said that he had been in two of my classes, first as a freshman and two years later in British Literature as a junior. He laughed and remembered that he had failed at least one of those courses because he recalled having to go to summer school to make up the credit. He didn't believe that he had done much better in the other.

I replied that I regretted to hear that, and he reassured me that the fault was entirely his since he had never completed assignments nor passed in research papers and the required essays. I used to remind my students that if they didn't give me anything to evaluate, I had no grade to give them. I told him that I rarely, if ever, failed anyone who demonstrated some degree of effort.

"Don't sweat it," he replied.

And then to my utter amazement, he began to recall our study of an "unusual poet with a unique style who ignored punctuation, capitalization, and sentence structure -- just scattered his words every which way down the page, even coined new words like 'mud-luscious' and 'puddle-wonderful' - something like that."

"e. e. cummings," I said, identifying the writer of this unconventional free verse.

"Yeah, that's him," replied my repairman.

Then he mentioned our study of *Romeo and Juliet*, about two star-crossed lovers from feuding families, although I don't know that he named them -- Montague and Capulet. What he most clearly could visualize was the balcony scene in which Romeo, while hiding in the garden beneath Juliet's balcony, secretly overhears her musings in which she professes her love for him. Leaning her chin upon her hand as she speaks, Romeo ardently sighs, "Oh, that I might be a glove upon that hand, that I might touch that cheek." My former student recalled riding in a truck with a teen friend -- the friend's girl seated in the center, lodged between them. The young man had his arm draped around his girl, fingertips trailing her arm. "Mr. Repairman" was sweet on the girl himself, and he associated what he was observing in the truck with his own desire, much like Romeo's yearning to touch Juliet. It was years since we had read the play in class, but at that moment in the truck those lines finally resonated with him.

Next, he recalled a lesson focused on examining newspaper headlines for connotative words that are deliberately employed to influence the reader's opinion even before he has read the article.

In that instant, I blurted out my repairman's name. "Yeah, that's me," he acknowledged.

"Oh my!" I responded incredulously. "You've remembered ALL THAT from so long ago."

"Yeah," he agreed, "I can't believe it either."

"Well," I apologized. "If I could go back and change your grade, I certainly would. You've made my day."

A teacher really never knows whether or not her words are falling on fertile soil, planting seeds that will eventually blossom. In this case the lessons took root and remained with him long after graduation.

"So what does all of this have to do with this collection of book reviews?" you might ask.

Well, the teacher in me remains and so does my desire to share great literature.

"A teacher never loses her class," it is said.

That is why in my retirement, I write book reviews for the local newspapers in Rhode Island and do presentations at the local library and to women's groups in Ft. Lauderdale, Florida where I spend the winters. It is my way of sharing books that are too good to miss -- that will entertain, enlighten, educate, and stimulate your imagination. Some are about historical events, some about different cultures, others about interesting individuals. They are my favorites; I sincerely hope they become yours as well.

FICTION

The occasional extra space or hyphen
was the result of a faulty computer disc
and should not interfere with the reading.
A recent reprinting has corrected this
in future copies.

THE GOLDFINCH

by

Donna Tartt

An intriguing and unusual story, *The Goldfinch* begins with a terrorist bombing of a New York City museum which 13 year-old Theo Decker and his mother are visiting prior to an appointment with the headmaster at Theo's school nearby. Just before the explosion, mother and son become separated because Theo's attention is drawn to a pretty, delicate red-haired girl walking hand-in-hand with an older man, her Uncle Welty and guardian whom the boy had begun to follow. In a split second, all is chaos, falling debris of metal and shattering glass, smoke, fire and burning. In a semi-conscious state, Theo sees the old man, fatally injured, reaching toward him and pointing to a small antique painting of a goldfinch.

Crawling among wreckage to reach the elderly Welty, Theo tries to comfort him; but in his final moments Welty is talking wildly of someone named Hobie at a certain address to whom the boy should bring a signet ring which he gives him. In his rambling, he also instructs Theo to "take the painting away from here."

Once Theo is able to escape the wreckage without being noticed, he finds his way home, dazed and traumatized. There he hides and waits for his mother to return, although sub-consciously he realizes this is not likely. Eventually he is found after his mother's death is confirmed, and social services place him temporarily with the family of a friend, Andy Barbour. This begins another layer of the plot involving the dysfunctional Barbour family, who will reappear throughout the book. Later remembering the old man's instructions, Theo makes his way to the address given by Welty and is taken in by Welty's partner Hobie who deals in antique furniture restoration. There he finds the red-haired sprite, Pippa, recuperating from her near-death experience in the

1

bombing of the museum. They find comfort in each other, having experienced the same trauma and loss. However, this friendship is soon aborted when Theo's long-lost father arrives to take custody as does Pippa's aunt. Life with Theo's alcoholic dad, who is also a gambler, is lonely and unsupervised; and soon Theo finds himself shop-lifting, drinking, and getting high with a new friend Boris. They heavily indulge in all kinds of drugs; and added to Theo's post- traumatic stress, he becomes an extremely troubled and lost adolescent, hopeless and depressed.

When his father has a fatal accident following threats by mobsters to whom he owes money, Theo flees back to New York where he arrives at Hobie's doorstep -- hungry, ragged, and ill. There he is taken in, the only place, other than with his mother, where he feels totally accepted and cared for. Gradually he learns the antique business through his mentor and becomes very knowledgeable about the distinctions between Chippendale, Duncan Phyfe, William and Mary, Queen Anne, and the rest. With this expertise, how-ever, and without Hobie's knowledge, he begins to make a small fortune sell-ing these reproductions and restorations as authentic pieces. All this time he has kept the valuable painting of "The Goldfinch" a secret and hidden from everyone.

Nevertheless, in one drug-induced, wild night he shares its where-abouts with Boris, who keeps coming into his life at random times. When Theo realizes Boris has taken the painting, he follows him to Amsterdam to retrieve it. Much of the rest contains pages upon pages of heavy drug use by both, run-ins with underworld characters, shootings, chases, philosophizing about the nature and beauty of art and one's relationship to it, the purpose of life, the effects of loss, etc. I cannot say that Theo finds himself throughout any of this; his is a journey of pain, loss, loneliness, deceit, yearning, self-loathing, and an obsession with a painting that is always inextricably associated with the mother he adored and her love and appreciation of art.

THE LIGHT BETWEEN OCEANS

by

M. L. Stedman

Heart-rending. Poignant. Moving. Such is the novel *The Light Between Oceans* by M. L. Stedman. The setting is a bleak and isolated lighthouse on Janus in Australia to which the stoic and laconic keeper, Tom Sherbourne, brings his new wife Isabel to live. Izzy's gaiety and spirited nature have enabled Tom to overcome the post-traumatic stress disorder and depression he suffers following time spent fighting in WWI. But life in this lonely and wind-swept location affects Izzy adversely, particularly following two miscarriages, in addition to the loss of a stillborn son. Until one day a lost skiff carrying a dead man and crying infant washes up on their tiny isle. Izzy strongly believes that this baby has been sent by God and is overcome by a maternal love so strongly pent up while carrying her own babies. Tom, on the other hand, feels it is his duty to report to the authorities on the mainland the arrival of the man and the child, but his wife convinces him to wait. As he witnesses the instant bond between Izzy and the child and how it transforms his wife, he is hesitant to do what he knows is right and allows Izzy to persuade him to bury the man and keep the baby. Finally, they have the family for which they both have been yearning and allow themselves to love and nurture this little girl whom they name Lucy. Although Izzy seems able to live with this, the fact that Tom has not properly reported the facts, nags at him and overshadows their bliss. When Tom is allowed shore leave after his three year stint as the lighthouse keeper, the little family returns for a vacation to the mainland where events force them to recognize the consequences of their decision. This is an emotional story which left me crying for pages. It is also a well-woven plot, which you will find suspenseful as the two well-rendered characters -- Tom and Izzy -- become immersed in the lives of others on the mainland -- all through their connection to this child. This is a real page-turner -- not a book you will quickly forget.

THE ART FORGER

by

E. A. Shapiro

For those art aficionados, as well as those who enjoy a good mystery, you will find *The Art Forger* by E.A. Shapiro highly entertaining, as well as extremely informative. As well as weaving together a suspenseful and engaging plot, she provides so many accurate details about art history, painting techniques, famous artists, and -- most interesting -- how the art (and it is an "art") of forgery is accomplished. The main character is a talented, but unheralded painter named Claire who, in order to rescue her depressed artist boyfriend from of his funk of long duration, takes one of his unfinished works and completes it as he lies on the couch observing her and occasionally offering suggestions. Upon completion, the painting is heralded as his very best work -- a masterpiece -- that boosts his reputation to new heights. Claire's contribution remains secret and unacknowledged. But the main plot involves an art dealer named Markel who brings her what he asserts is one of Degas' famous masterpiece series entitled "After the Bath," missing for years following its theft in the 1990 heist at the Isabella Gardner Museum in Boston. Claire may not be well-known, but she is an expert on forgery since she is engaged in legitimate reproduction work of masterpieces for interested buyers. She recognizes "After the Bath" for the fake that it is and through diligent research, realizes that no connoisseur has ever recognized it is a forgery in all the years at the Gardner Museum. Eventually, Claire falls in love with Markel, which complicates things immensely. As she creates a reproduction of the forged "After the Bath," she does not share with him her certainty that this painting is a fraud. The best feature of this book is the very intricate description, step-by-step, of the process of forging a piece of art. First, it is necessary to locate a painting from the same time period because the canvas will be stripped down to its sizing and laboriously prepared to take the reproduction. Claire has studied a master Dutch forger from the early twentieth century, Han van Meegeren who

5

invented this process -- painting the new one over the old to "maintain the craquelure, then using formaldehyde as an additive to harden the paint, then baking each layer to desiccate the paint so it is as dry as it would have been after centuries, further aging the painting with a final wash of India ink and tinted varnish." After the completion of this task, she hands over the painting to Markel who, in return, has promised her own "one woman" show at his gallery; but he is arrested before that can take place. Now the plot deepens, since Claire could reveal the fact that Markel never had the original Degas in the first place, which might exonerate him from culpability. Furthermore, after additional sleuthing, she is convinced she knows where the real Degas might be hidden. This is a provocative story on many levels. There is a great deal of theorizing about authenticity -- whether a "great" forgery is, nevertheless, a great painting; also what is the "real" motive for collecting and owning art? Is it an aesthetic appreciation for the work itself, or is it a selfish desire to own and hoard what others cannot have. What about the thousands of struggling, extremely talented artists who might indeed be superior to the "star" of the moment, but never achieve recognition? *The Art Forger* combines a most engaging, cleverly inventive and thrilling plot with meticulous research of art history; I highly recommend it.

NORWEGIAN BY NIGHT

by

Derek Miller

An 85 year-old widower, Sheldon Horowitz has moved from the US to Norway to live with his beloved granddaughter Rhea and her hus-band Lars. Rhea is concerned that since his wife's passing, Sheldon seems to be suffering the beginnings of dementia. What Rhea does not know is that her grandfather has been struggling a lifetime from intense guilt regarding his ac-tions as a Marine sniper in The Korean War. In addition to this heavy burden, Sheldon is convinced that he was also responsible for the death of his son Saul (Rhea's father) in Vietnam. He feels that his comments about the war and his Jewish heritage affected Saul's decision to enlist. Much of the story takes place in Sheldon's mind as he recalls scenes from the past, particularly conversations with his late wife and with fellow soldiers who did not return from war. He has recurring nightmares about his best friend Mario who was blown up right in front of Sheldon's face. He has fantasies of accompanying his son on a danger-ous mission, even visualizing again and again his violent death. One day while alone in his daughter's apartment, he hears a terrifying altercation between an unknown assailant and the female neighbor living in the flat above them. When she flees and seeks refuge with her little boy, he allows them in and attempts to lead them away to safety, but the mother is killed and he escapes with the child. Her death is the result of her actions during the war in Serbia where she photographed Serbian violence designed for ethnic cleansing. Throughout a lifetime Sheldon has experienced a great degree of personal and emotional conflict regarding various wars in which he was engaged -- Korea, Vietnam, WWII, and Kosovo. Much of it is all mixed up and confused in his memory, but when he becomes solely responsible for the life of this child who is being sought by his mother's attackers, he becomes lucid enough to out-smart them.

Relying on his instincts and former training as a soldier, he cleverly foils all attempts to capture the boy. This makes for a very suspenseful thriller, taut with tension as Sheldon and his charge stay only steps ahead of their pursuers, as well as the police whose aid his granddaughter has enlisted to find her grandfather. This is a very skillfully written novel with deep psychological insight into the soul of a tortured man who finds himself in alien territory at both the beginning and end of his life.

KEEP QUIET

by

Lisa Scottoline

One split-second decision. That's all it takes to turn Jake Buckman's life and that of his family upside down. From the moment one dark night when he allows his son Ryan, who only has a driver's permit, to exchange places with him behind the wheel for a short trip home, their lives are changed forever. This is a suspenseful tale with many surprises, the type of mystery story for which *New York Times* best-selling author Lisa Scottoline is best known. Jake intended this gesture to help connect to Ryan who has become distant, but he could never have imagined the nightmare of lies and deception into which this would plunge both of them, as well as his beloved wife Pam. The plot begins when father and son leave the scene of an accident after finding a teenage girl dead, believing they were the cause. Their guilt, remorse, and anxiety are relentless during the days following when they attempt to set things right and own up to their actions. Both are legally liable, and each is willing to sacrifice his life in prison for the other, but Ryan refuses to let his father take the blame. What complicates matters is that Pam is nominated that same week for a prestigious judgeship, an honor and position for which she has striven all her years on the bench. This will require intense investigation of the entire family by police, the attorney general, as well as the FBI. Jake and Ryan's anguish, depression, and fear are so well-described by the author as to feel almost palpable to the reader. Your heart races with theirs as they are questioned by the police; you are sickened as they are when they need to pass the spot of the accident with its makeshift memorials placed by the victim's classmates; you become distressed too when they realize their actions have jeopardized Pam's entire career for which she has worked so diligently. Haunting their every moment is the realization that if they confess, Jake could spend years in prison and Ryan in a juvenile detention facility, ending all hope of going to college on

9

a basketball scholarship. Their final decision will be affected by many factors: a blackmailer who witnessed the "accident," a predator stalking the teenage victim, her affair with the high school coach, and Pam's unexpected actions to sacrifice her career in order to save her husband and son. You will not be disappointed by this page-turning novel with its many twists and turns, culminating in a very satisfying conclusion.

OUR SOULS AT NIGHT

by

Kent Haruf

Short, simple, and sweet -- but, oh, so very sweet! Such is Kent Haruf's final book, *Our Souls at Night.* The recipient of so many awards including The National Book Award, The Whiting Foundation Writer's Award, and The Wallace Stegner Award, to name just a few, Haruf passed away in 2014. I love his direct, concise yet eloquent style.

Using the common give and take of dialogue, he is able to convey in his unique manner, intense depth of feeling -- regret, sorrow, and yearning. There is a sparseness in his writing; nothing is superfluous, somewhat like Hemingway. But despite the absence of sophisticated words and language, his simply constructed sentences succeed in telling his narrative with humanity and keen emotional power. One of the main characters is Addie Moore, a lonely widow who craves companionship and human connection, who out of this need reaches out to Louis Waters, a neighbor widower. She is neither coy nor ambiguous when she suddenly knocks on his door one night with a proposition. If he is agreeable, she will welcome him into her bed each night for talk and friendly conversation. Although surprised, he too is lonely and agrees to her suggestion. And so during the dark hours, they discuss their childhood, former spouses and marital relationships, their children, their unfulfilled dreams -- in the most forthright and honest manner. Both find comfort and solace in this newfound arrangement, until Addie's adult son becomes aware of it and threatens to limit her time with her grandson who has been staying with her while his parents are separated. He does not realize that the boy has formed a very close bond with Louis who has been a healthy influence and comforting presence to the bewildered child and a close confidant to Addie as well. This is tragic because this narrow-minded, mean-spirited son has created an awkward wedge which thwarts their poignant camaraderie. I have been a fan of Kent Haruf since reading an earlier novel *Plainsong* characterized by the same sparse style and quietly focused on exploring our shared humanity. In that story it was the non-judgmental and unconditional acceptance of two elderly bachelor brothers -- rural farmers -- who take in a pregnant girl with nowhere else to go. I recommend both books highly and regret that we will have no more compassionate tales by this exceptionally gifted and gentle man.

THE DINNER

by
Herman Koch
(Translated from Dutch)

The narration of Herman Koch's very unusual story takes place entirely during the courses of a dinner at a very high-end restaurant which has been selected by Serge Lohman, candidate for Prime Minister of Holland, who is there with his wife Babette, brother Paul, and sister-in-law Claire. The chapters are in sections titled "Apertif," "Appetizer," "Main Course," "Dessert," and "Digestif." During the narration, extreme and undue attention is paid to the ingredients in each dish served: Greek olives from the Peloponnese lightly dosed with extra virgin olive oil from Sardinia; lamb's neck sweetbreads served with arugula and sun-dried tomatoes from Bulgaria; lasagna slices with eggplant and ricotta; "vitello tonnato"; and finally a "dame blanche," for dessert. This food has absolutely nothing to do with the unsettling and bizarre tale being told, except that the maître d' keeps interrupting the conversation among the Lohmans to provide a detailed and belabored description of each item ordered, much to the annoyance of all. Of course, the author intends this as a spoof of ultra-sophisticated culinary snobs. The tension mounts steadily throughout the meal as the conversation turns to discussion about their children who have become involved in a horrendous crime.

Both sets of parents disagree as to how best to handle the situation. It becomes apparent that violent hostility and animosity have always existed between Paul and his brother Serge, and this problem perpetrated by their boys exacerbates it to a taut pitch. Each set of parents is not aware of how much the other set knows of the details and who exactly was at fault. Paul's anger increases as he surmises that Serge is more concerned about the scandal ruining his chances in the upcoming election and also resents that Serge and Babette once attempted to remove his son from his custody when Claire had to be hospitalized many years ago (cause left unknown to the reader). That is only one of the mysteries here as well as secrets that unfold a bit at a time. We learn that Paul is filled with anger, prone to violence, has had his own psychological breakdown, and that much of his rage and jealousy is directed at his brother. This is not a bland story and the characters are somewhat twisted. From the start the reader is aware that Paul is not entirely stable and relies on his loving and beautiful Claire to keep him steady, but then the author switches gears unexpectedly. Is she the loving, dutiful, nurturing woman whom Paul has portrayed? There is also an element of speculation as to what tendencies a child inherits from his parents as they try to figure out what went wrong raising their son. This is one book that will keep you guessing: Why all the emphasis on food? Is Paul just weird or mentally unbalanced? And what about Claire who began as the most likeable and genuine character? Moreover, is anything entirely resolved at the end?

SONGS OF WILLOW FROST

by
Jamie Ford

Set in Seattle, Washington in the late 1920s and early '30s, *Songs of Willow Frost* begins at Sacred Heart Orphanage on William Eng's twelfth birthday; in fact, it is the communal birthday -- a date chosen by the headmistress Sister Briganti to celebrate those of all the children at the institution. Part of the festivities is a trip to the cinema downtown to see a movie. Although William has not seen his mother in five years, he is almost certain that the actress, Willow Frost, whom he sees on the screen is his mother, whom he used to call Ah-ma. Back at Sacred Heart he shares this belief with his best friend Charlotte, a blind child who like him, yearns for her mother. Together they form a very close bond, and encouraged by her urging, they flee in hopes of finding William's Ah-ma. This is a poignant story of suffering and sacrifice, longing and disappointment, abandonment and reunion. William will find what he has been searching for -- not only his mother but the reasons for her leaving him, and it is a tale tinged with sorrow and regret. The author focuses on the sad situation of children during the Depression, who for various reasons, became wards of such orphanages, which despite the misguided intentions of the caretakers, could be lonely, cold, and harsh environments. Your heart goes out to these well-rendered characters -- William, his Ah-ma Willow, his friend Charlotte -- as they face adversity and try to take control of their lives. The author creates a very realistic setting when Book-mobiles had just begun bringing books to readers, when silent movies were being replaced by talkies, and when adoption and state agencies ignored the rights of single, unwed mothers and took control of their offspring. Although it is a story from another time period and another place, it centers on the bond between mother and child which is elemental and eternal.

THE LITTLE PARIS BOOKSHOP

by

Nina George

"The little Paris bookshop" is actually a barge on the Seine which Monsieur Perdu has chosen as his location for *la pharmacie litteraire* or *Literary Apothecary.* A ramp from the boat to the shore allows his patrons access to the bookseller. His main purpose is NOT to sell books, however, as much as to select the books for his customers depending on what ails them. Through his books, he treats afflictions of the soul. What a novel idea! In the very first chapter, he refuses to sell a certain book to a distraught woman because he believes it will do her more harm than good. The book the woman was seeking was written by Max Jordan, a young man suffering writer's block, who will eventually become the "son Perdu never had." When Max inquires of Perdu as to why he did not sell the woman his book, Perdu replies, "Booksellers don't look after books; they look after people." What Max is yet to learn is that Perdu himself is suffering an "affliction of the soul" having been abandoned by Manon, the love of his life. As a result, angry, disappointed and depressed, he has shut himself away in a single room for many years in an attempt to avoid getting too close to anyone else. All of this will change when, impulsively, after finally bringing himself to read the letter left by Manon so many years ago, he puts his barge to sea to find the village to which Manon returned.

This book screams Paris with references to the Eiffel Tower, Champs Elysees, Place de la Concorde, Montmartre, the Sorbonne, Notre Dame, The Pont Neuf, Galleries Lafayette (where I recall being treated badly, totally ignored by the receptionist in "The Information Booth" where I asked directions! I could go on and on about the indignities suffered at the hands of the French, but that is a story for another piece). There is romance and passion here, as well as mystery. Why did Manon leave her beloved Dupre? What was in the letter he refused to read for twenty years? If you are a Francophile or biblio-phile, you will enjoy this enchanting novel which has been called "a love letter to books." For more than a year, it has remained on "Best-seller" lists in Italy, Poland, Germany, and the Netherlands.

THE GIRL ON THE TRAIN

by
Paula Hawkins

The Girl on the Train is one exciting, heart-thumping thriller about Rachel Watson who is at the nadir of her existence, having lost her husband Tom, her home, her job -- her entire life -- as a result of chronic drinking. Cathy, a kind and sympathetic friend, has offered her a room but is unaware of her unemployment since Rachel takes the train from the suburbs into London every morning pretending to go to work. On that same route each day, Rachel has the opportunity observe from the window the lives of others, particularly when the train slows and stops at a signal. One couple who interests her she names "Jess" and "Jason," but whose real names are Megan and Scott. She assumes that they are happily married, envies their interaction as she frequently sees them cozily having breakfast on their deck above the tracks. It is understandable that she fantasizes about other people because she has no life of her own. In addition, she regrets her unpredictable and ugly drunken behavior which she believes was responsible for the break-up of her marriage and still yearns for her "ex" Tom. To add to her distress and self-loathing, Tom has remarried a woman named Anna and they have a child Evie. Unable to get on with her life, Rachel harasses both Tom and Anna with frequent phone calls and stalking behavior, particularly when she is on a binge. Even her closest friend Cathy is losing patience and respect for her because in her stupors, Rachel is often unconscious, disheveled, ungroomed, vomits on the carpets, and leaves her bedroom and the kitchen a mess. It is in one of these drunken states, that she takes the train out to the suburbs one night to see Tom and Anna and can't remember how she returned home injured -- blood on her hands, gash on her skull. For weeks she struggles to remember what happened that night, but it is lost to her as a result of the frequent blackouts she is experiencing. In an attempt to regain some part of her memory, she consults with

19

a psychiatrist whom she recognizes as the man she saw kissing Megan while passing by on the train one day. She is suspicious because she knows Megan is married to Scott, but nevertheless she finds herself attracted to the doctor. To add to the mystery, Megan disappeared on the same night Rachel went to the suburbs. Rachel has this nagging, uneasy feeling that she was witness to something violent involving Megan, but is trapped in this hopeless darkness. In this story, there is one surprise after another, the author constantly veering from one possibility to another, misleading the reader, provoking tension and arousing suspense. When will Rachel remember what she saw and what part she may have played in it? Read this riveting tale to find out the answers.

CUTTING FOR STONE

by

Abraham Verghese

An avid reader, I am amazed that somehow I missed this superb novel when it was published in 2009! One of the very best books I have ever read, *Cutting for Stone* takes place in Ethiopia and focuses on twin brothers, Marion and Shiva Stone, conjoined at the head and separated at birth. Their mother, an Indian nursing nun, dies in childbirth; and it is assumed that their father is Thomas Stone, the dedicated British surgeon whom their mother assisted in a primitive, make-shift hospital in Africa for seven years. When Stone became ill, suffering a breakdown from exhaustion and overwork, she cared for him; and it was probably during that time that they became intimate. However, the author leaves this shadowed in mystery, and the reader is uncertain that this was the case. After the nun's passing, Dr. Stone, distraught and unhinged, disappears; and the twins are raised by a couple who are both doctors at the clinic.

Under the guidance of these loving and stable parents, both boys are introduced to medicine at a very young age. Another significant character is the girl Genet with whom they grow up, who will wreak havoc in the brothers' relationship. It is because of her that Marion will flee to America where he immerses himself in the study of medicine to alleviate the pain she has caused him. Shiva, on the other hand, will remain in Ethiopia where he will become a famous expert on female gynecological problems resulting from girls being married off too young. In the meantime, their father, Dr. Stone, becomes a renowned expert on organ transplants at a prestigious Boston hospital, and it is only by accident that Marion will come in contact with him there. *Cutting for Stone* contains a plethora of medical information, the natural result of the profession these characters share, but it flows so seamlessly from the plot that it does not pose a problem for the reader. Moreover, these are complex individuals with personal and relationship issues. There is conflict aplenty between the brothers themselves, as well as their feelings of abandonment by their father. At the end a serious illness will bring them together forcing all to deal with these lifelong realities from which they have made every effort to escape. In addition to a gripping plot is information about how the medical system works in the US where medical students from undeveloped countries are encouraged to immigrate in order to fill the vacancies in the poorest, underfunded hospitals which American doctors shun. This is a truly beautiful tale of the enduring power of the bond between siblings, despite their best efforts to deny and sever that connection. It is a moving and poignant testimony to the triumph of brotherly love.

MRS. SINCLAIR'S SUITCASE

by

Louise Walters

The title refers to a suitcase Roberta's father John brings into "The Old and New Bookshop" where his daughter works. It contains old books belonging to his 109 year-old mother Dorothea who is now living in a British nursing home. In the bottom of the luggage belonging to her grand-mother, Roberta finds a puzzling letter dated 1941 from a Jan Pietrykowski telling Dorothea that he cannot forgive her "for what you do to this child and this child's mother which is beyond honor." He expresses his ardent desire to spend the rest of his life with her, but "now their friendship must end." But as far as Roberta knows, her grandmother was married to Pietrykowski, so what does this strange message mean? The chapters alternate between Roberta's modern day life and that of her grandmother Dorothea's in the English countryside during WWII. Each chapter begins with some stranger's random letter which Roberta finds sometimes tucked between the pages of these used books brought to the store to sell. They offer a peek into the lives of other people, which interests 34 year-old Roberta who has little life of her own. But the missive that intrigues her the most is the one written by Jan Pietrykowski. In an attempt to solve the mystery, she tries to question her father, who is evasive; her elderly grandmother Dorothea, who is no longer always coherent; and Suzanne, the attendant/caretaker who spends the most time with Dorothea. Gradually, in the chapters devoted to Dorothea's life will emerge a story of multiple miscarriages, despair at not having a child, her rape by an abusive husband, a romance with a handsome Polish pilot -- all interwoven with two young girls, Aggie and Nina, government farm workers who board with the young Dorothea and play an important part in the novel. This is a good read about disappointment in love, family secrets, the results of duplicity, and irrevocable decisions all set against the background of war.

23

GO SET A WATCHMAN

by

Harper Lee

      Many readers eagerly anticipated this second novel *Go Set a Watchman* by Harper Lee, acclaimed author of *To Kill a Mockingbird*, but it is not of the same quality. Although set in the same location (Maycomb, Alabama) with some of the same characters, Atticus Finch and his now- adult daughter Scout, (brother Jeb has died), it lacks the emotional impact and suspense of Lee's first novel. When the story begins, Scout is home for a visit from New York City where she now resides. At the depot, she is met by Hank, her father's protégé and assistant who has had a crush on Scout since childhood. There is a lot of flirtatious banter between the two, with Hank making repeated proposals and Scout fending them off with assertions that she is too independent to make a suitable wife, yet she seems very fond and comfortable with him. Reverting to their childhood behavior, she races him for a jump in the creek, followed by a long ride to their favorite old natural haunts. Despite her grown-up status, Scout is constantly reminded by her Aunt Alexandra, who has replaced Negro housekeeper and much-loved nanny Calpurnia, to act like a lady, dress properly, and mind her manners. Finding these expectations restrictive and old-fashioned, the recalcitrant Scout ignores them completely. However, in her father Atticus' eye, she can do no wrong and theirs is a mutual admiration society. Until one day she follows him to the courthouse where he had, so long ago, defended the innocent black boy accused of rape. From the balcony she had watched with intense pride Atticus' eloquent defense which won the boy an unexpected acquittal. However, this time she witnesses her father discussing current issues with ignorant racists intent on limiting the Negroes' present status in Alabama. She even recognizes some former Ku Klux Klan members mouthing the most heinous bias against the black race. In a single moment she loses all respect for the father she has so idolized, so sickened that she goes outside to vomit. The rest of the story has her angrily attacking Atticus' principles and seeking desperately for understanding of her father's changed stance. Nearly hysterical, she vows she never wants to see him or Maycomb again. It is a violent rejection of all she holds dear; and in a direct confrontation, replete with animosity, disgust, and loss of illusion, she calls him a hypocrite and worse. There are many pages devoted to the merits and abilities of blacks versus Whites, and Atticus attempts to make her recognize that blacks, given years of enslavement and lack of education, may be pushing too hard for advancement, although not quite ready to lead themselves. This is anathema to Scout who is reeling in disbelief. If you desire to read how all this is resolved, I invite you to pick up this long-awaited novel. One of the advantages of having seen the movie *To Kill a Mockingbird* is that while reading *Go Set a Watchman*, I constantly and easily visualized Atticus as the actor Gregory Peck who played the role. Reading this novel will put you in familiar territory.

EMPIRE FALLS

by

Richard Russo

Story telling is an art and Richard Russo is a masterful storyteller, particularly in his Pulitzer Prize winning novel, *Empire Falls*. Its locale is typical of other Russo novels, an old mill town whose waters have been polluted by wealthy, exploitative factory owners who have drained the town and its inhabitants dry before moving on to greener pastures. In this case it is the Whiting family; and as in some of Russo's other novels, the setting itself becomes a major character, as if personified and peopled by all the off-beat or eccentric individuals found in such a locale. No one captures the essence of small town America better than Richard Russo.

The main character is Miles Robey, who, despite his mother Grace's most fervent efforts and wishes, has never made it out of Empire Falls where he seems eternally stuck in the dead-end job of managing a local diner owned, of course, by a member of the Whiting family. Actually, the Whitings have played a significant role throughout Miles' entire life, some of which is a mystery it will take him a life-time to figure out. There are secrets here, as well as passion, infidelity, loveless marriages, disappointment, dashed hopes, revenge, retribution -- all played out in this predominantly blue-collar back-water. In addition, there is plenty of clever irony as well as some laugh-out-loud funny scenes. In one there is an elderly, senile parish priest who has absconded with the Sunday Mass collection, along with Miles' derelict, shiftless, and irresponsible dad with whom Miles has an uneasy relationship. The priest is seen hearing the confessions of drunken patrons at one end of a seedy bar in, of all places, Key West where the pair has fled after stealing the rectory car. Russo weaves a very intriguing and entertaining novel with myriad characters whose lives intersect and overlap through multi-generations and culminates in a shockingly gruesome ending. Empire Falls is the type of place the author knows only too well; unlike Miles Robey, however, Russo managed to go beyond its narrow and limiting perimeters. He deserved to. His talent as a writer was his ticket out.

STONER

by
John Williams

The famous writer-philosopher Henry David Thoreau once wrote, "Most men lead lives of quiet desperation," and William Stoner, the main character of this book, is one of those individuals. Born on a farm in Missouri to poor parents, Stoner expects that he will have no choice but to follow in his father's footsteps when, in 1918, he has the unexpected opportunity to attend agricultural college. The expectation is that once he has his degree, he will return to the farm and employ the new techniques he has learned. But sometime in his second year he becomes enamored of the written word, the beauty of language, and a sense of wonder in prose and literary phrases that emotionally resonate deep within him.

And so he becomes a teacher of literature and finds fulfillment and release in the classes he instructs. The powerful works of Chaucer, Milton, Jonson, Bacon, and Shakespeare engage his mind and excite him. However, there are times when his reticence and timidity do not allow him to convey this to his students and he feels disappointed in himself. A loner, he has few friends, just an uneasy, superficial relationship with his colleagues. But his awareness is heightened when he meets Edith Bostwick and falls hopelessly in love. Their brief courtship is painful to read since it is fraught with the uncertainty, hesitation, and awkwardness of two people who really do not know each other. Soon after marriage, their relationship becomes strained and tense. This is not a book of action, but rather one of repressed but passionate feelings. Stoner reminds me of the character Ethan Frome in Edith Wharton's novel by that name. Like Ethan, Stoner is trapped in a loveless marriage to a controlling spouse and is ineffectual in expressing his dissatisfaction and disappointment. Also like Ethan, Stoner will have one opportunity to escape, but a sense of duty and responsibility will thwart his desires, leaving him with a fleeting sense of what might have been. Both are admirable men of integrity, but overwhelmed by their circumstances. Beneath what appears to be a slow-moving tale of a man's struggle to find meaning in his life, there is an intensity of emotional turmoil and scenes of unbearable inner conflict. At the end, despite a sad and difficult life, as well as an undistinguished career, Stoner emerges a hero, something like the elderly fisherman in Hemingway's *The Old Man and the Sea,* who despite having lost the biggest catch of his life, returns to land with the carcass, a symbol of his success. Both Stoner and Hemingway's old fisherman are glorious in their defeat. This is one powerful, extremely well-written novel, revealing in its psychological depth and eloquent in its simple, quiet style.

GONE GIRL

by
Gillian Flynn

WOW! *Gone Girl* is one page-turning, twisted tale with too many shocks and surprises to mention. In some respects, it is similar to the psychological thriller *Fatal Attraction*, except that in this case the two main characters, Nick and Amy, are a married couple. Their relationship, much of which is described in Amy's diary entries, begins in mutual passion and love; but during its five year duration deteriorates in a wildly disturbing manner. Amy is an egotist, possibly the result of her parents' depiction of her as the heroine in their highly successful children's book series entitled *Amazing Amy.* She has grown up believing "their press" -- that she is indeed incredible -- incredibly beautiful, creative, clever, and smart -- all of which she demonstrates in this story, but in extremely bizarre ways. For example, she requires that Nick demonstrate traits she deems necessary for the "perfect" husband, so that he becomes, in a sense, a puppet on a string with her as the manipulator, wielding complete control. When she feels that he fails in this mandatory role she has created for him, she becomes bitter and resentful. As a result, she begins an elaborate, psychopathic plan to teach him a lesson. The diary technique using Amy's first person narrative is most effective in revealing character. This is a deliberate ploy on Amy's part, as well as a brilliant tool in setting up her husband, but "sick" in the most dangerous and sinister ways. This is a well-written, absorbing novel -- dark suspense at its best.

Lest I spoil this gripping mystery by giving away too much, I recommend that you read this chilling portrayal of an extremely disturbed woman and her machinations to keep her husband marching to "HER" drummer. You won't be disappointed.

NIGHTWOODS

by

Charles Frazier

Nightwoods, the most recent novel by Charles Frazier, author of the "Best-seller" *Cold Mountain,* is set in rural Appalachia where the main character Luce has retreated to a solitary and isolated existence. Hers has been a hard life, abandoned by her mother, raised by a cruel father Lit, and bereaved following the death of her only sister Lily. The only consolation for her sadness and loneliness is the natural beauty and quiet of the lake and the blue-green mountains that surround her. She is a child of nature, keen to the chirping and soaring of the birds, the changing landscape through the seasons; it comforts and sustains her. She has only two elderly friends: one, old Stubblefield whose ramshackle "Lodge" she cares for, and Maddie, a reclusive, but kind woman who also inhabits the wooded glen. Suddenly, Luce's peaceful life is upended by the arrival of her deceased sister's children, twins -- a girl named Dolores and a boy named Frank. Silent, morose, and uncommunicative, both appear to be emotionally damaged. The only witnesses of their step-father Bud's attack on their mother, they have withdrawn into their own private world. Although Bud was acquitted at his trial, Luce suspects that the children harbor paralyzing fear from his traumatic assault upon their mother.

Feeling totally inept at raising children and meeting with skittish withdrawal each time she attempts to interact with them, she is reduced to simply feeding them, allowing them to run free outside, and getting them to bed. They will not allow any physical contact, nor allow bathing. The siblings seem to have a mutual understanding. Eventually two other characters influence the lives of all three: a younger Stubblefield who inherits his grandfather's "Lodge" in which Luce and the kids live, and Bud, the husband of her late sister Lily. Stubblefield is touched by these strange children and is carrying a torch for Luce from high school days, although she has changed drastically from the pert

33

and pretty high school cheerleader and beauty queen whom he remembers. Bud, on the other hand, is intent on finding ill-gotten money, taken and hidden from him by Lily, of which he believes Luce and the children are aware. To make matters worse, Bud becomes friends with Lit, Luce and Lily's step-father, an equally unscrupulous, violent, and dangerous partner. Read this odyssey -- for that is what it is -- of Luce's introduction to motherhood, of the children's healing under her care, of Stubblefields's rekindling of young love, and of the avenging of Lily's death -- all set against the natural Appalachian landscape which Frazier depicts so well in his beautiful descriptive prose. One example: "Her hair changed color several times a year, like leaves on deciduous trees." Although this work is not quite as gripping as Frazier's masterpiece *Cold Mountain*, he still maintains his command of sensory appeal which is one of his greatest talents. "Bright migrant finches, yellow and black, darted for the last droplets of withered blackberries ... yellow sunbeams ... and flowers thick in the yard -- coneflowers and gladiolas and black-eyed yellow Susans -- all dangling together in late summer -- air sweet with the smell of crushed stalks heaped in bright yellow piles and the boiling molasses syrup and wood smoke ... amidst the grinding of the cane press and the occasional pop of the hickory fire." This is a most enjoyable read -- not only for a well- woven plot, but also for Frazier's delightful and creative use of imagery throughout.

THE SOUND OF GLASS

by

Karen White

An unusual and somewhat bizarre mystery, *The Sound of Glass* focuses upon the Heyward family, beginning with the matriarch Edith, an abused wife who secretly builds miniature replicas of crime scenes in the attic of her house. They are painstakingly reproduced with miniature papier mache copies of furniture, room layouts, and human figures often positioned in their final poses. From her father, a detective, she learned to be a keen observer of even the most minute detail. The purpose of her staged reproductions is to help the local police in solving mysteries. One which has remained unsolved is that of a 1955 plane crash which occurred over her Beaufort, South Carolina home, leaving debris strewn everywhere. When she finds a piece of luggage in her garden, Edith carries it into the house to examine it. Along with the clothing inside, she finds a letter addressed to "Beloved." The strange and shocking contents of that letter will enable her to put together the puzzling crash scenario, but for her own reasons she keeps all to herself. Instead, she takes one of the ties and mails it to the wife of the name on the luggage tag because she feels a kinship with this woman whom she has learned by the letter has, like Edith, suffered abuse. The plane crash also led to Edith's husband's death since the distraction and shock it caused on his drive home resulted in his fatal accident. The tale will continue through the raising of her son and then her two grandsons, Cal and Gibbes, after their parents' deaths. Eventually after her own passing, the house is inherited by Cal's widow when the story shifts to a new set of characters: Merritt, Cal's widow; Cal's brother Gibbes who is nothing like Cal; Merritt's young step-mother Loralee (also widowed), and Owen, Loralee's 10 year-old son, as well as Merritt's younger brother whom she has never met. At the beginning of the story, all these characters and their relationships to each other seem very confusing, but the reader does well to stick with it because as the story progresses, it all becomes clear.

Following Merritt's father's remarriage to the much younger Loralee, Merritt and her father never reconciled. Loralee, the step-mother, has her own reason for suddenly bringing Owen to meet his unknown half-sister.

Merritt, a very conservative, insecure, and vulnerable New Englander, has always resented Loralee for taking her father away and despises her step-mother's brash, seductive style, teased hair, and Southern drawl. In addition, Merritt is infuriated by Loralee's maddening habit of repeating *ad nauseum* tidbits of wisdom which she prefaces with "As my momma always told me..." But Loralee has a big heart and beneath all that hair is a country, homespun understanding of people and empathy for them, Merritt in particular.

Although this may all seem difficult to follow, the author Karen White, despite spinning a somewhat convoluted plot, has cleverly incorporated many surprising twists and turns at every bend. Some of the coincidences on which she relies while developing the story may strike the reader as a bit too contrived or seem unbelievable. Nevertheless, it has redeemable qualities. It is a well-written story of facing fear, overcoming inhibitions, forgiving, letting go, and starting anew.

A SPOOL OF BLUE THREAD

by

Anne Tyler

For *A Spool of Blue Thread*, which Pulitzer Prize-winning novelist Anne Tyler has declared her last novel, she has chosen three generations of the Whitshank family as her cast of characters and their family homestead as her setting. The house itself plays a prominent part in this story, almost becoming a character itself as it draws all the various relatives to this location. It has been the one fixture in all of their lives.

Originally built by the grandfather Junior in the 1920s, it has now passed down to his son Redcliff and wife Abbey, who like Junior and his wife Linnie Mae, have raised their family in it. Now all four of Red and Abbey's grown children have returned since both parents are demonstrating signs of illness and deterioration due to aging. It soon becomes apparent that jealousy and resentment have always existed between the two sons, Denny, who is Red and Abbey's biological child, and Stem, who was adopted. Denny is angry that Stem has taken it upon himself to move into the Whitshank home to supervise the forgetful and ailing parents, but to Stem it seems only natural that he should assume the responsibility since he has worked all his life by Red's side in the family construction business. Denny, on the other hand, has been a drifter without a permanent home, address, or job, rarely in contact with anyone. After Abbey dies, Stem learns that she has kept secret the identity of his real mother all these years. He is angry, shocked, and ashamed because she was not a woman respected by the Whitshank family. He also learns that Abbey, a former social worker, compelled his mother to sign a contract giving up all claims to him. Denny, on the other hand, is struggling with his own feelings of inadequacy and lack of acceptance, since his father always seemed to favor Stem for his maturity, responsibility, work ethic and superb craftsmanship. This is a tale of family, the relationships between brothers and sisters, the hurts and failures of the various members, the carefully crafted and guarded image parents sometimes try to create. It is also about letting go, particularly of a home which has symbolized so much to the various generations.

Originally it was treasured by the grandfather for the stability and prestige it afforded him after so many years of toil, a tangible sign that he had "made it." For Red and Abbey, it represented the permanence and stability of their love. Early in their relationship she had said, "Red, I want to learn every step of you, and dance till the end of the night." And for their children and grandchildren, it was a place to come home to, a haven, a refuge. Since the place each of us calls "home" is such an essential and formative part of our lives, this story is likely to resonate with many readers.

THE LAST SUMMER AT CHELSEA BEACH

by
Pam Jenoff

Pam Jenoff, the author, deliberately creates a very specific sense of place in her latest novel, *The Last Summer at Chelsea Beach*, since all the action that influences the young characters in this novel takes place at this summer resort in New Jersey. It is 1941 and teenager Adelia Montforte has just arrived from Italy, where her parents, fearing Fascist imprisonment, have whisked her away under cover of night to smuggle her to America where she will live with her Jewish aunt and uncle. These relatives spend summers at a Chelsea Beach bungalow adjacent to an Irish family, the Connallys which includes four young boys: Liam, Robbie, Jack, and Charlie. Adelia ("Addie") makes fast friends with the entire brood, including parents, and becomes part of the family. It is the eldest Charlie -- popular, handsome, and athletic -- to whom she is most at-tracted while Robbie, the youngest, seeks her as his playmate. Jack becomes very protective, and the brooding Liam seems bent on self-destruction with his wild antics and rebellious companions. The tragic events of one summer will change all of their lives, splitting them apart, some to distant corners of the world. Despite relocation the trauma will follow them. This is a story of young love, loss, mistakes, war, sacrifice, redemption, and making choices. Like another Jenoff novel, *The Winter Guest*, some events in the plot seem unlikely. In this book the author relies a bit much on coincidence; for example, when Addie flees to England following the tragedy to which I allude, she will run into Charlie who is now a soldier.

Much later after she has returned to the US and goes to collect items from her aunt's beach bungalow, she will reconnect with Liam who is restoring the Connally house in an attempt to atone and bring his family back together. Despite the coincidences that slightly strain credulity, this book successfully evokes a certain time and place and will hold your interest.

WHAT WE KEEP

by

Elizabeth Berg

Much of the narrative in *What We Keep* is told from the point of view of 12 year-old Ginny, whose mother Marion has abandoned her family which includes her husband Steven and their other daughter Sharla. At the beginning of the story in the 1950s, the Young family appears solid and stable until a new neighbor, Jasmine, moves in next door. Compared to their own traditional, conservative, stay-at-home Mom, Jasmine appears exotic, alluring, daring, and exciting. But her arrival will trigger an upheaval in this family since each member is greatly influenced by this newcomer's style and ideas -- none more so than the mother Marion.

What the girls and their father have not noticed is that beneath the veneer of normal family life, Marion, in the restricted role of homemaker, has been struggling with her own frustration, unhappiness, and lack of fulfillment. Although dutifully performing tasks expected of a wife and mother at that time, she craves more satisfying outlets of expression. As usual, the author Berg focuses on the many facets of relationships -- that between husband and wife, between parents and children, between sisters, as well as new friends. This is a compelling, emotionally wrenching story, particularly when Berg details the painful feelings of young girls rejected by their mother. The author is best when writing about sensitive interactions between her characters, focusing on the heart of the female -- her longings, needs, and desire for intimacy.

CHESTNUT STREET

by

Maeve Binchy

Ardent fans of the prolific and beloved Irish novelist Maeve Binchy with many "best-sellers" to her credit, will be disappointed to learn that *Chestnut Street* is her last work. Ms. Binchy died in July 2012 in her native Ireland, the setting of most of her books. *Chestnut Street,* however, is not a novel as much as a collection of vignettes whose characters are the residents of the various houses on the street. One is a taxi driver who overhears a lot during the time he drives people to and from Chestnut.

Another is Liberty Green, who despite her name and her parents who talk about *The Rights of Man* and have a copy of *The Declaration of Independence* in a prominent place on the wall, is over protected and allowed little freedom. As she grows up, she yearns for some distance.

Then there is "Bucket," the window washer, so called because he travels to various jobs on his bicycle from which dangles his bucket. His greatest disappointment is that due to animosity with his ex-wife, he has not been allowed frequent access to their son whom he loves dearly. When the boy turns out badly and is in danger from thugs, Bucket sacrifices himself for his son.

There is the brusque, friendless Gwendolyn whose penny-pinching ways allow no enjoyment of life or appreciation of camaraderie and beauty.

There are a number of mothers opposed to their child's choice of a spouse for various reasons, as well as husbands and wives engaged in secret affairs.

Such is the stuff of any community and Chestnut Street is no exception: love affairs, disappointments, unwanted pregnancy, concern with appearances, inheritance issues, desire to get ahead, hard-working blue-collar laborers, family estrangement, blind dates, empty-nest syndrome -- all that constitutes the everyday lives of ordinary people.

The chapters alternate among these various characters who do interact on some occasions. Otherwise, the technique used is that of separate short stories that focus on some noteworthy event in the person's life, some turning out rather ironic. In these vignettes, Binchy allows the reader a glimpse into their psyche -- their motivations, their feelings, their choices. One street in Ireland is the center of it all.

NB: Although this was the last of Binchy's novels, a collection of formerly unpublished short stories entitled *A Few of the Girls* came out posthumously in 2016.

THE GREEN ROAD

by

Anne Enright

A book about family dynamics, *The Green Road* focuses on the dysfunctional Madigans -- the mother Rosaleen and her four adult children who have left their home in western Ireland for other parts of the world. Dan, the gay son, has moved to New York where he indulges his homosexual proclivities with many partners, yet always unable to connect emotionally in any meaningful way. His brother Emmett has been working as a missionary in Africa while their sister Hanna has become an alcoholic. These siblings also have relationship issues. The only one who has remained close to home is another sister Constance, who married a local man and is raising a family. Now their mother summons them home for a last Christmas in the family homestead which she has decided to sell. All these characters seem to be harboring his/her own degree of bitterness and resentment. Rosaleen feels her children blame her for not doing a better job as a parent since none of them has amounted to much in her eyes or that of the world. (There seems to be no ill will toward the father who has died). All four recall their mother, when young, as a hypochondriac using her health as a tool to manipulate them when they disappointed or opposed her, withdrawing to her bedroom for days rather than facing unpleasantness. Now they don't believe that she really intends to sell their childhood home, since in the past she has never been able to act directly on anything. Her style is to skirt around issues, deny, hide, procrastinate in an attempt to avoid confronting reality or dealing with what must be done. They find her irrelevant chatter about trivialities maddening, as does the reader, when so much of the anger and fury burning within all of them needs to be addressed -- vented in some constructive manner. Instead, on this Christmas Day when they are finally all together physically, but as emotionally apart as ever, Rosaleen runs from the house into the cold December weather and becomes lost. She too is angry that all have left her with seldom a letter, visit, or phone call, making her feel that she "doesn't exist, doesn't matter." When she fails to return, they search frantically for her and realize that although they do NOT like their mother, they DO love her.

This newly released book has garnered a lot of attention possibly because the author Anne Enright has won a number of awards: The Man Booker Prize for her novel *The Gathering,* as well as The Andrew Carnegie Medal for Excellence for *The Forgotten Waltz*. Despite the fact that she was named the Inaugural Laureate for Irish Fiction in 2015, I do not feel this particular work is deserving of such honors. For one thing, the dialogue, with its uncompleted thoughts, leaves the reader hanging in the air. I suppose that is deliberate since much of real speech is sometimes left unfinished as the person drifts off into thought. Moreover, there are sentences containing little of substance; for example, one goes on for lines listing all the various foods sitting on the holiday table. Its only purpose might be to emphasize how Rosaleen herself can only focus on trivial details but not real issues. For those readers who have an interest in abnormal psychology, this family might serve as an intriguing subject.

THE HIRED GIRL

by

Laura Amy

What a refreshing book and charming protagonist! *The Hired Girl* refers to 14 year-old Joan Skraggs who, after the death of her beloved mother, flees her loveless home ruled by a tyrannical and emotionally abusive father. She is found on the streets of Baltimore by a kind young man who brings her home to his Jewish family, the Rosenbachs, where she becomes the "hired girl." In this cultured and elegant home, her real life will begin, despite the fact that she is merely a domestic. For one thing she will have access to the family library teeming with the classics which will inspire her in her primary ambition to become a "noble and refined person with only lofty thoughts."

Embarrassed by her extremely hard-scrabble beginnings, limited education, and lack of class, she is so earnestly bent on self-improvement that often her efforts to are so "over-the-top" as to become amusing. She so yearns for "dignity, sophistication, and poise;" to know how to use a "well-turned phrase;" to forego "giddy pleasures," so that she will no longer be an ignorant farm girl. The many books she obtains in the Rosenbach library will enable her to better express herself by using phrases she encounters in her readings; she recalls that beauty can "ennoble and edify" and she so wants that for herself; she "aches with indignation" and sometimes "feels affronted" or "abashed;" she begins to refer to the city as an "imposing metropolis;" her heart is often "overcharged and seems to swell;" a "rapturous tempest stirs in her bosom;" she feels the need to be more "formally attired" but then remorsefully chastises herself for "accursed vanity." (I just love the quaint phrasing! She begins to model herself after heroines she admires in novels: Jane Eyre (by Charlotte Bronte and Florence Dombey (from Charles Dickens so as to emulate their "courage and resolution." She is enthralled and enchanted by everything to which she is exposed -- opera, art, architecture and fashion -- so much so that

47

her innocence and naiveté are endearing. Even her hesitation to mention "indelicate subjects," such as changing the bed sheets or asking directions to the ladies' room, are amusing.

A 2015 Newberry Award Winner, *The Hired Girl* is an excellent choice for young readers as well as adults, since it is a "coming of age" tale told in diary format which provides insight into the heart of the main character as she vacillates between elation and despair, depending upon her daily experiences. In addition, for the art enthusiast, each of the seven sections of the book is introduced by a classical painting or engraving aptly chosen for the contents of that particular chapter: "Girl Reading" (Winslow Homer), "The Warrior Goddess of Wisdom" (Michelangelo), "The Maidservant" (W. A. Breakspeare), "Mariana in the Moated Grange" (J.E. Millais), etc. This is one girl's delightful odyssey -- complete with romance and enlightenment, hope and aspiration that ends with her typically melodramatic line: "Tomorrow, oh tomorrow! What will my destiny be?" I loved this book and recommend it highly.

THE JAPANESE LOVER

by

Isabel Allende

The Japanese Lover focuses on Alma Belasco whose parents send her to her aunt and uncle in America when the rise of Hitler threatens their safety in Europe. In her new home she becomes close to her cousin Nathaniel and closer still to Ichimei, the son of the Japanese gardener.

Alma is heartbroken when Ichimei and his family are relocated to internment camps following Japan's attack on Pearl Harbor. Although they write back and forth to each other, much of the contents of Ichimei's letters are blacked out due to heavy censoring by the government.

Despite years of separation, they remain in love and never forget each other, although both will marry other people. The other main character in the book is Irina Bazili, an abused girl with a sad past, who becomes Alma's caretaker at the nursing home where Alma resides in old age. Irina and Alma's grandson Seth will become allies in seeking answers to the mysterious letters and gifts sent to Alma there. Both are very curious about secrets from her past which she has kept hidden from all but her deceased husband.

This is a story of enduring passion and devotion that spans a lifetime, despite the odds being stacked against the lovers. Actually, there are two romances Allende develops in this novel since Seth has fallen in love with Irina who keeps him at a distance due to her own traumatic scars. Like the older Alma and Ichimei, this couple is also separated but in a different way -- by Irina's secret past that keeps her from giving herself to Seth.

Hovering over the story as an aura of mystery and secrets which Allende creates with the lyrical prose for which she is well-known.

WE ARE NOT OURSELVES

by

Matthew Thomas

We Are Not Ourselves has been described as "an American middle-class epic" spanning three generations. As such, it follows the life of Eileen Tumulty beginning with her upbringing in an Irish family in which both mother and father are heavy drinkers. It is from their lower-class background and dreary, cramped apartment that she dreams of escaping, which seems possible when she meets and falls in love with Ed Leary, a research scientist. She believes that together they can rise in life to a better house in a better neighborhood. This is of prime importance to Eileen, although it gradually becomes apparent that her husband does not share this desire. He seems content to stay at his teaching job, willingly passing up higher-paying positions that Eileen wants him to take. While he is content to remain in the original house where they began their life together, Eileen's ambition to own a fine home in the suburbs becomes an obsession. She is convinced that only in such a place will she find happiness and fulfillment. Through relentless maneuvering, she convinces Ed to make the move, but it still falls short of her high expectations. No matter what improvements they are able to afford, it is never quite enough to bring it up to her standards. Her very frugal husband, who insists on doing the renovations himself, seems resentful of the time, cost, and burden imposed upon him, and it is not long before his health begins to fail. Owning a lovely home is a major part of this story; it seems that having grown up in one she loathed where she always felt deprived has driven Eileen on this quest for "the perfect house in the perfect neighborhood" where all will be sunny and bright. It is really an impossible dream -- unrealistic to think that any abode will satisfy all one's desires. This is also a story of a marriage that, although not perfect, is based on real love. Moreover, it is the tale of stressors in the Leary's marriage and the toll they take on the whole family, which includes a son Connor. In

51

addition, it is a hard and sobering look at a family struggling with early onset Alzheimer's, combined with the caretaker's guilt, sacrifice, conflict, fear, fatigue, and frustration that accompanies such an illness. At the end, it is ironic that Eileen returns to visit their original home which another family inhabits. To her utter surprise, it seems they have imbued it with the warmth, contentment, and coziness that has always escaped Eileen. Perhaps the theme is that the so-called American dream of home-ownership, and the status and satisfaction derived from it, can be a dubious quest; since it is not the "HOME" itself that insures contentment, but those who inhabit it.

WHAT WAS MINE

by
Helen Klein Ross

What is a mother? She who gives birth to you? She who loves, raises and nurtures you? She who supports you physically and emotionally for twenty one years? These are the questions facing Mia, the main character in this book, who struggles with the dilemma of determining exactly who she is. Born to Marilyn and Tom who named her Natalie, she is raised by single mother Lucy under unusual circumstances which I don't want to reveal for fear of spoiling the suspense of the story. The trauma of the loss of their child causes Marilyn and Tom such stress as they react in different ways to the sorrow, that they eventually divorce from the strain. Marilyn is convinced that their Natalie is still alive out in the world somewhere; while Tom, also in shock and grief, attempts to move on. Eventually Marilyn will heal to some degree, remarry, and have three more children. In the meantime, Mia (originally named Natalie) is enjoying life with Lucy, the only mother she has known. Lucy is a high-powered career woman so Mia is usually in the care of Wendy, a sort of Chinese au pair who observes her first steps, takes her back and forth to school daily, cooks her meals and supervises her homework. Mia probably spends more time with Wendy than Lucy. The chapters alternate between both major and minor characters, such as Lucy's sister Cheryl. Each gives his or her perspective (from the first person point of view) on the strange circumstances of Mia's disappearance at age four months, as well as on the other characters in the story. Some will be more forgiving and sympathetic than others; and the tale will be revealed through their personal assessments of the individual who wreaked this havoc on so many lives. This is a "fascinating psychological study of motherhood" as Lucy lives with a terrible secret. Later in the book you will find that Wendy too has her own secret. This very good book will reveal the disastrous results of one woman's selfish act and its tragic repercussions on many other people close to the situation.

THE OTHER DAUGHTER

by

Lauren Willig

Rachel Woodley has always believed her father, a botanist, died in a remote location when she was four years-old. At least that is what her mother told her and Rachel has warm memories of a loving dad who tossed her in the air, played with her, soothed her, and doted upon her. When she is suddenly summoned home from London where she works as a governess, she senses that something is drastically wrong and arrives too late. Bereft from the death of her mother, Rachel is further shocked to find hidden a society page newspaper article and photograph of a Lady Olivia Standish shown on the arm of her father, the Earl of Ardmore. Comparing old pictures of her together with her parents, Rachel is certain that this earl looks uncannily like her own father, although older. Impelled by her overwhelming desire to know the truth, she makes her way to his country home intending to confront him. But first she must make her entrance into an elite and stratified society closed to commoners. For this to happen, she is assisted by a handsome but suspect journalist who covers the society world and is willing to be her escort. Together they compose a false identity for her which they hope will be convincing enough to achieve their end. Of course, Rachel is jealous and resentful of this "other" daughter Olivia who somehow replaced her in their father's affection for more than twenty years. The plan is to become friends with Olivia in order to gain entrance to the family estate. But as with the well-known phrase by the Irish poet Robert Burns, "the best laid plans ... oft go astray." Rachel is surprised to find that Olivia is not at all what Rachel expected. This is an entertaining story with an engaging plot. Rachel is set on getting answers, but initially they are not the answers she so desperately wants to hear. Many of her preconceived notions about both her father and her half-sister Olivia are turned upside-down, and there is an unexpected outcome involving the unknown journalist.

THE NEST

by
D'Aprix Sweeney

Family inheritance, which is the subject of *The Nest* often brings to the surface long-held, dormant emotions in siblings -- rivalry, feelings of favoritism by parents, comparisons of professional and financial success in adulthood, and concern about receiving bequests of equal value. The siblings in this case are members of the dysfunctional Plumb family: Jack, who is living with his gay partner Walker; his brother Leo, the black sheep of the family; their sister Bea, an insecure and unsuccessful writer; and the ever-anxious and overprotective Melody, the mother of twin girls. "The Nest" refers to a vacation home their deceased father bought initially as an investment for his children's future, a sort of insurance in case of emergency, with the condition that it would not pass to them until Melody, the youngest, reached forty. Without their knowledge or agreement, their distant and usually uninvolved mother has chosen to use funds from the sale of "The Nest" to cover the medical and legal expenses of a waitress, the passenger in an auto accident with the drunken Leo at the wheel. This expenditure greatly reduces the shares of the others, resulting in shock and anger. For many years, each has counted on this "nest egg" for various reasons: Melody, for her twins' college tuitions: Leo, to live on when he divorces his extravagant wife who has spent all his money: Bea, for an apartment of her own: and Jack, for repayment of loans he has taken behind Walker's back. Sweeney, the author, who intended the focus of her book to be about family, was surprised to learn that readers feel it is about money. At present, it has been on "Best-seller" lists for many weeks and has garnered a lot of attention here and abroad. There are also a number of sub-plots -- one involving a stolen antique found at "Ground Zero" by a fireman in the aftermath of 9/11. Another devolves from a budding lesbian relationship one of Melody's daughters is having with a teenage friend. Given its current popularity, one

57

might reasonably deduce that family inheritance and all that it involves is a topic which interests many people. I believe selling rights for a movie is currently under consideration.

HISTORICAL FICTION

VILLA AMERICA

by

Liza Klaussmann

Villa America is a well-rendered account of the lives of certain members of "the lost generation" living abroad on the French Riviera during the 1920s. At the center of Klaussmann's intricately woven, multifaceted plot are a married couple, Sara Wiborg and Gerald Murphy, actual Americans who, following very lonely childhoods, found happiness and acceptance in each other. Completely absorbed with their newfound love, they married and moved to the South of France where they built a lavish and elegant residence, "Villa America," to which they invited guests to share their luxurious, playful, and somewhat hedonistic existence: sunbathing, boating, and swimming in the azure Mediterranean waters; picnicking on its sandy beaches; elegant and sumptuous dining; excessive drinking and wild evening soirees were enjoyed by all. Visitors included famous author Ernest Hemingway and his wife; Zelda and F. Scott Fitzgerald; artist Pablo Picasso; Archibald and Ada MacLeish; playwright Philip Barry; writer Dorothy Parker, and other famous "literati." The close proximity that "Villa America" afforded them, as well as the fiery debates and exchange of ideas that ensued, often stimulated their writing. In fact, Fitzgerald used his hosts, Sara and Gerald Murphy, as the prototypes for the main characters, Dick and Nicole Diver, in his immensely successful work *Tender Is the Night.* As one might imagine, the gathering of so many greatly talented people, who brought with them their unique eccentricities and mammoth egos, often made for intense conflict and heightened emotions which comprise the events in this story. Klaussmann has done extensive research on the Murphys, initially focusing on them as subjects for her Master's thesis. As the author tells it (occasionally through actual letters exchanged across the Atlantic), the Eden-like atmosphere the Murphy's created and delighted in for many years could not last forever. As one poet so concisely but accurately said,

"Nothing gold can stay"; and so eventually the Murphys will experience their share of tragedy and heartbreak, which makes for very intense reading. We are offered a glimpse of the relationships and marriages of a group of very creative but complicated people, as well as a view of the golden Grand- Epoch era and its glamorous lifestyle that is gone forever and can only be imagined.

GEORGIA

by

Dawn Tripp

The "Pioneer Painter" who lived in the desert painting brilliant New Mexican flowers, stark white cow skulls, granite canyons, fleecy clouds, wet blue skies, soaring mountains, river valleys and red hills -- the wild beauty of the rugged Western landscape. A phenomenally talented artistic photographer she sought out in New York who became her lover, mentor, and eventually her husband. These are the subjects of this book: Georgia O'Keeffe and Alfred Stieglitz who was obsessed with this female painter using her as a model for his highly erotic, evocative, sensuous nudes, "explicit and unrestrained." In the 1920s, they were considered an extraordinary couple, the old photographer and his young artist/muse whose abstracts were also considered revolutionary -- her union of form and color a "new American art." Theirs was an extremely passionate affair, but also tempestuous, given his penchant for flirting with other women. Nevertheless, he was dedicated to showing her work in galleries, his exhibitions making her well-known. Despite Stieglitz's keen appreciation of Georgia's talent and his devotion to her career, in the early days of her career she felt it necessary to please him, creating works that he believed would be welcomed by the public. In addition, when she read the reviews of the critics -- all male -- she often felt her art misunderstood. As a result, there was always an inner struggle between "doing her own thing" and conforming to his judgment of what was worthy of exhibition. Another source of contention and disappointment was her desire to have a child and his refusal to give her one. Alfred believed that the demands of motherhood would distract her from her art which was to be fostered at all costs.

Eventually resentment builds to the point where she will leave him in New York for long periods of time to seek her own artistic and personal fulfillment in Santa Fe. Here she feels most at home in the pueblos among high mesas surrounded by desert air. This atmosphere and location is essential to her artistic productivity. It renews, rejuvenates, re-inspires her. More signifi- cant is that here she can be herself, follow her own whims and inclinations without restriction or restraint. She thrives in the Navajo territory where the "sun rises over soft gray hills that give way to red cliffs." She finds peace and inspiration in riding horses through flowing streams, the wind blowing through her hair. At last she frees herself of male influence; her success as an artist a personal victory that is hers alone.

The story is told from the "I" point of view, which gives it a personal quality so that the reader is better able to feel Georgia's conflict and struggle for independence both as a woman and an artist. In addition, the author suc- ceeds in conveying the depth and intensity of passion between the two main characters. However, the writing style too often follows an elementary sub- ject-verb pattern which sometimes becomes monotonous. In all, I would rec- ommend this book to those interested in gleaning information about Georgia O'Keeffe, her life, her work, her relationship with Alfred Stieglitz; but if you are looking for soaring, sophisticated, dazzling language you will not find it here.

ALL THE LIGHT WE CANNOT SEE

by Anthony Doerr

A superb book -- compelling. engrossing, suspenseful -- in competition for The National Book Award, of which it was extremely deserving. Set in war-torn Germany and France during the 1930s and '40s, this book focuses on two main characters: a young, blind French girl, Marie-Laure LeBlanc, living in Paris with her father, a keeper of keys at the Museum of Natural History; and Werner Phennig, a young boy growing up in an orphanage in Germany with his sister Jutta. Both siblings are very close as are Marie and her father, but the rise of Hitler and Nazism will upturn their worlds volcanically.

Since Werner has an amazing adeptness with radios and transmitters, he is enlisted first in a Nazi Youth Group and sent to be educated in Berlin. The cruelty and sadism he witnesses at the academy for the most gifted of German youth, appalls and horrifies him; but he soon realizes that to show compassion is to bring attention to himself as a weakling, leading to derision, torture, expulsion, or worse. One of his closest friends is so mercilessly beaten when he refuses to follow the commandant's brutal order, that he is physically and mentally damaged for life. A basically decent and moral adolescent, Werner is overwhelmed with unjustifiable guilt for not having done enough to shield his companion, although it would have been permanently injurious to himself as well.

While Werner is becoming more and more skilled at building radios, fixing them, and breaking codes, Marie accompanies her father daily to the museum where French curators are feverishly labeling, packing, shipping, and hiding valuable paintings, artifacts, and jewels in anticipation of Nazi invasion and plunder. Among these precious items is a rare gem, of which three copies are made. One is entrusted to Marie's father to keep hidden for the duration of the war, although he does not know whether the one in his possession is authentic or fake. Eventually Marie and her father must flee Paris and seek refuge with an eccentric relative in St. Malo. During their dangerous and terrifying trek, the reader is anxious for their safety. From this point the story becomes increasingly urgent. The reader's heart races with theirs as they barely escape discovery and escalates as Marie and the agoraphobic, reclusive uncle, who takes them in, become involved in transmitting secret messages to aid the Resistance. Although blind, Marie is chosen as the least obvious suspect in going to the local bakery each day on the errand of buying a loaf of bread which contains a slip of paper with secret written codes.

From a cramped attic room, her uncle will relay this information to the partisans. There is so much suspense and excitement in this story as the father teaches his handicapped daughter how to navigate the city. In addition, the author is clever and imaginative in the manner which she creates for hiding the gem. The alternating of chapters, between a day in Marie's life followed by a day in Werner's world, creates a very effective parallel narrative. Moreover, the historic content heightens the reader's awareness of the unbearable hardship, adversity, challenges, and agonizing horror endured by those who were victims of the conflict and carnage. Even Werner, a German officer, is an unwilling participant, coerced into assisting in the Third Reich's madness for world domination. What he is forced to do goes against every grain of his character and eventually destroys him. Not only is this an extremely moving tale, fraught with danger and suspense -- difficult to put down -- but it is also a statement about the loss, waste and utter futility of war.

THE NIGHTINGALE

by Kristen Hannah

Historical fiction, *The Nightingale,* focuses on two sisters with very different temperaments living in France during WW II. Isabelle, the much younger sibling, is feisty and rebellious, having been expelled from a number of schools for disobedience and infraction of the rules. Vianne, the older sibling, has never been close to her and often looks with disapproval upon Isabelle's behavior as flighty, selfish, and immature.

Upon the death of their mother, their non-communicative father sends them away from Paris to the family country home, "Le Jardin," in the Loire Valley where they are supervised by a governess/housekeeper. While the younger is transferred from school to school by her disinterested father, Vianne marries and remains at "Le Jardin" with her husband who soon enters the army. Upon the Nazi invasion of Paris, the father sends Isabelle to live with her sister, but the two are so alienated, their life together is a series of bickering and quarreling. Soon their town is invaded and the family home is requisitioned by a young and very handsome German officer. Unable to tolerate this, Isabelle leaves to join the partisans by distributing leaflets encouraging resistance. Eventually she becomes more deeply involved and assumes the very dangerous role of helping downed Allied airmen escape across the border. At times she must seek asylum and lodging with her father in Paris, but he is not pleased to see her and tries to reject her as always. In the description of the hardships and deprivations of war, the anti-Semitism, the movement of displaced Jews to concentration camps, the resulting torture and suffering, this book echoes *Sarah's Key* and the more recent *All the Light We Cannot* See. This story is compelling and suspenseful as danger surrounds them everywhere and secrecy is paramount (even their father has his own secrets). Through their war experiences, all three will grow to a better understanding and acceptance of each other's flaws and limitations so that each is able to forgive and finally demonstrate love for one another. All three will be sorely tested and forced to make irrevocable choices that will forever affect their bodies, souls, and psyches. In some instances, they will have no choice as they are all victims of the ravages of conflict. Usually war is men's business, but in this book, the author focuses on two women.

ALONG THE INFINITE SEA

by

Beatriz Williams

In this, Beatriz Williams' most recent historical novel, the setting alternates between Germany and France in the 1930s, and Cocoa Beach and Cumberland Island (USA) in the 1960s. What links the two together is the auction in Palm Beach of a rare 1936 vintage black Mercedes-Benz belonging to Miss Pepper Schuler, one of the female protagonists, to new owner Annabelle Dommerich, the other female protagonist in this story. This chance acquaintance will pair the young unmarried but pregnant Pepper with the older widowed Annabelle, who will provide support as well as a haven for Pepper as she seeks anonymity on the run from the powerful and well-known politician who is the father of her unborn baby. What occupies Pepper's curiosity is why Annabelle would seek out this particular car and pay such an enormous price for it. What she does not know is that this vehicle enabled Annabelle, her Jewish lover Stefan, and children to escape Nazi Germany. There is romance aplenty in this plot as well as danger and suspense, secrets and sacrifices, betrayal and revenge. As the story unfolds we learn the intricacies of Annabelle's complicated past, including marriage to Johann, a high-ranking Nazi military man from whom she, like Pepper, attempted to escape many years earlier. There are surprising twists, one early on when Johann, the strong and well-intentioned rescuer, first offers marriage to the young and pregnant Annabelle when abandoned by Stefan. But not all is as it appears, nor are some of the characters what they seem. One in particular will shock you with his reversal. This is a good read, although some of the incidents are a bit far-fetched and coincidental. Nevertheless, it is a well-paced book focused on rescue in various guises.

THE GARDEN OF LETTERS

by

Alyson Richman

Love, war, death, tragedy, intrigue, suspense, and secrets are all part of this compelling historical novel, *The Garden of Letters*, by national best-selling author Alyson Richman. Set in Italy during World War II is the tale of a talented young cellist, Elodie Berlotti, who becomes caught up in the German invasion of her native Verona. After her beloved father is arrested and beaten nearly to death, she becomes involved in the Resistance to thwart their Nazi enemies. Her very unique assignment is to convey messages through codes worked into the musical pieces which she performs before audiences. In this way, vital information is hidden and conveyed through her music to those whose ears are attuned to decipher it -- a very clever technique employed by the author in the weaving of her plot. Communication without words is a major theme of this novel and is further developed through Elodie's romance with Luca, another Resistance fighter by whom she becomes pregnant. Their encounters are fraught with ever-increasing tension as they must both elude SS officers as they carry out their missions. Danger and brutality lurk all around them as they must summon all their resources to escape detection. At one point, Elodie flees by boat which delivers her to Portofino, a lovely small resort town. When upon disembarkation she is delayed by guards who demand to see her forged papers, Angelo, the town's physician, suddenly and unexpectedly appears to claim her as his cousin. Angelo, who saves her from imminent arrest, has his own tragic background which will be revealed in bits and pieces. This is a story of heartbreak and irretrievable loss, of lives shattered and repaired by finding love again, of despair transformed into hope. There is also music in Richman's tale and its beauty and ability to transport and soothe broken souls. This is good storytelling.

LISETTE'S LIST

by
Susan Vreeland

If you are what the French call "une amatrice d'art," (passionate lover of art) or even a just a dilettante, *Lisette's List* by Susan Vreeland, author of *Hyacinth Blue*, is likely to appeal to you. Set in the countryside of Provence during World War II, it involves a young couple, Lisette and her husband Andre, who move from Paris to the small village of Roussillon, to care for Andre's aging father Pascal. At first Lisette is disappointed with their new location; it is very primitive, a tiny, drafty, stucco house without indoor plumbing or any other amenities. In addition, the small town lacks the fun and sophistication of Paris with its cafes, nightclubs, and museum galleries of fine art. But what it does have is the very lovely Provencal countryside with its endless undulating fields of lavender, its quaint ochre colored stone cottages, quaint windmills and water wheels, creamy yellow smokestacks, leafy orchards of leaning olive trees, and the rich loamy smell of the earth. Moreover, its very unique brilliant light, the delight of artists for centuries, is like no other place in the world. Having been there myself, I can attest to its natural beauty and bucolic landscape. Soon Lisette becomes enchanted with her new home and particularly fond of her father-in-law, Pascal. He acquaints her with stories of his work in the nearby quarries where he labored with a pickax to extricate the ores from which the paint pigments were made. She is awestruck to learn he had personal interactions with Camille Pissarro, Paul Cezanne, and Marc Chagall with whom he bartered pigments for paintings. On the crude walls of this humble abode hang their work -- seven in all. Eventually, Pascal dies and Andre enlists to fight the Germans who have conquered Paris and are now invading the countryside. His first priority, however, is to hide the valuable paintings; but he does not share their whereabouts with Lisette, feeling she is more protected in this way if the Nazis come looting. The remainder of the plot focuses on the loss of Andre, the danger in which Lisette finds herself alone and at the mercy of the Germans, her attempts to find the paintings at the end of the war, and her search to find love again. Also of interest are the theories regarding the importance and value of art. Lisette contemplates about what makes a painting great. Her conclusion is "its power to enrich us with truth, to enlighten us so that we understand our lives more clearly." I am by no standards a connoisseur, but I do dabble in painting, and for me it's the aesthetic sense that a fine work of art evokes from the viewer. The uninitiated, as myself, cannot actually pinpoint what exact quality it is that draws him to the painting; he only knows that in a sense it "speaks" to him in some inexplicable way. He may know nothing of brush strokes, value, or technique; but what he does know is that he is seeing deeply something exquisite or challenging or even indecipherable -- it has touched his soul, his imagination profoundly and he is richer for it.

THE WINTER GUEST

by
Pam Jenoff

Pam Jenoff's, *The Winter Guest,* is set in Nazi occupied Poland during WWII. When posted there for the State Department working on Holocaust issues, the author came up with the plot of a downed American airman (Sam rescued by a young Polish woman (Helena. To help him, Helena endangers not only her own life, but that of the family she is trying to support and keep together following the death of her father and hospitalization of her mother. Food is scarce and she scrounges the nearby forest for whatever is edible. In addition, she trades on the black market, which, if caught, is punishable by death. But her two young sisters, one a toddler, her 10 year-old brother, as well as her twin Ruth, are all dependent on her resourcefulness and leadership for survival.

Surrounding her are danger, destruction, and freezing temperatures. As she hides Sam in the ruins of a chapel in the forest and brings him whatever food she can obtain, their relationship blooms into a deep and committed love, exacerbating the strain that has always existed between Helena and her twin Ruth. At times Ruth fears that Helena will attempt an escape with Sam and abandon her and the children, but Ruth underestimates her sister's love and deep devotion to all of them. This is a story of the horrors of war and a romance that blossoms despite suffering, deprivation, and near death. It is a tale of betrayal and the ultimate need for forgiveness. Moreover, it is a story about making irrevocable, life-altering decisions in overwhelming, unpredictable situations. In addition, *The Winter Guest* is a well-written suspenseful novel, full of twists and surprises in a captivating, well-woven plot.

THE ORPHAN MOTHER

by
R. Hicks

A novel of historical fiction, *The Orphan Mother,* takes place in the years after the Civil War and focuses on a former slave Mariah Reddick, now free. An accomplished midwife all of her life, Mariah has brought thousands of babies, black and white, into the world in Franklin, Tennessee. Of course, the most important infant she has birthed is her own son Theopolis who has grown up with political aspirations. The South is changing, but not enough to allow an outspoken, ambitious black man to have his say. In 1867 on the steps of the court house where Theopolus is about to speak, he is attacked by a group of whites and beaten to death. Heartbroken, Mariah is intent on finding out why and who were responsible for his demise. This need to know will lead her on a trek of discovery that will have repercussions in the town of Franklin for years to come. This is a story of race and the human condition which still haunts us and remains with us long after slavery's end. It is also a tale of transformation since Mariah after a lifetime of bondage, although owner by a beneficent mistress, must undergo great psychological change to help her realize that she is no longer chattel subservient to the directions of others. She has a voice and she will use it to identify and denounce her son's murderers. In her efforts to avenge her son's death, she will have the help of her former mistress Carrie with whom she has an ambivalent relationship. Close playmates all of their lives, they share a background and history, having inhabited the same home as far back as either of them can remember. Mariah cared for this mistress throughout all of her pregnancies, helped her bury those babies that did not survive, and tended to her as both a friend and a servant. Another ally in the search for her son's assailants is Tole, a transplanted, former marksman from the Northern Union Army. A crack shot with a rifle, he has much blood on his hands and has been summoned to assassinate a political rival of a powerful town figure Elijah Dixon. This character will be skillfully and intricately interwoven into the plot involving Theopolis' death.

This is good story-telling set in a turbulent period in our nation's history. The heroine Mariah is a composite of the Southern Negro slaves who abruptly find themselves anchorless in a world for which they have had no preparation. Hers is a search for proper placement in this new environment, as is her son's as well -- a free black man with ambition and hope struggling to improve his own lot and that of his contemporaries. But he is too soon in his attempts and is cut down in the prime of his life. Given the racial tensions in present-day America, this is not an irrelevant story of the past, but resonates today in the daily news stories that focus on continuing hostility between negroes and whites.

MARRIAGE OF OPPOSITES

by
Alice Hoffman

     The setting for this novel alternates between Paris and the idyllic island of St. Thomas in the early 1800s. It focuses on the life of Rachel Pomie Petit Pizzarro, the mother of the renowned painter, Camille Pizzarro. Although an independent-minded young girl who consistently bristles at the rules and restrictions of her parents, she is made to marry a much older widower whom she does not love. With him come three children whom she begins to adore as well as some of their own born from this marriage. Upon his early death, she reluctantly moves back to her mother's home because a woman at that time was not entitled to inherit property. As a result, her husband's family sends a young nephew, Frederic Pizzarro from France to St. Thomas to manage the estate. So begins a most passionate and scandalous love affair -- frowned upon and considered incestuous by her Jewish community. Although deeply in love and desiring marriage, they are denied marriage in the church. Hence, they and their children are shunned, ostracized, and constant fodder for gossip. Defiant as always, Rachel will not succumb to regulation, and she petitions a higher church authority abroad. As a result, she and Frederic will be allowed to marry and their family will eventually consist of eleven children, the youngest and best-loved being Jacobo Camille. Headstrong like his mother, he is prone to conflict with her, mainly because of his artistic nature which she doesn't encourage. She would prefer that he work along with his father learning the family business. When both parents realize that Jacobo is not suited to this, they allow him to go to his father's family in France where he will pursue his artistic inclinations. This is a story of intense relationships, well-developed by the author who focuses on the passionate natures of her characters. The story is multi-layered in that initially, the focus is on Rachel's tense relationship with her mother who declares, "You never could accept that you were a woman and nothing more." Then the conflict switches to her adamant refusal to acquiesce to the strictures of the congregation regarding her marriage to the much younger nephew of her deceased husband. Simultaneously, the author is deftly developing other conflicts -- that of her sister-like friendship with Jestine, the daughter of her family's black servant. They grow up side by side, but their closeness will become strained when Jestine falls in love with Rachel's adopted brother who leaves her pregnant and goes to France.

When he returns with a wife, he takes their child away from St. Thomas leaving Jestine heartbroken and forlorn. But here is another intense conflict in that he is forever torn by his love for Justine and guilt-ridden by his abandonment of her. Add to all this an element of mystery since the circumstances of the brother's birth have been kept secret. So there are tiers and tiers of connected stories revealed in little pieces, but very assiduously woven in a seamless, free-flowing narrative. Moreover, are the issues of slavery, a woman's proper place in society, inheritance, desire to live on one's own terms, the nature of true friendship, parental control over adult children, the constrictions of society, the desire to pursue one's own dreams, and the basis for marriage -- multiple subjects, each worthy of a book in itself, but all dealt with in this masterful novel. In addition is the author's keen descriptive ability to create an Eden-like setting for the Caribbean island where much of it takes place. Hoffman does a noteworthy job of handling all these myriad elements presented in *Marriage of Opposites.*

THE INVENTION OF WINGS

by

Sue Monk Kidd

Sarah and Angelina Grimke, sisters from Charleston, South Carolina, were two of the first female abolitionists and earliest American feminist thinkers. Given that they were born into the power and wealth of an aristocratic family of slave-owners, such independent and liberal leanings were most unusual for women of their time. Active and vociferous activists in the anti-slavery movement of the 1800s, the Grimke sisters penned influential pamphlets and crusaded for both emancipation of slaves and women's rights.

It is surprising that they are relatively unknown today since both were on the public stage before Lucretia Mott, Elizabeth Cady Stanton, and Harriet Beecher Stowe, author of *Uncle Tom's Cabin*. Sue Monk Kidd, author of the best-selling novel *The Secret Life of Bees,* has made Sarah and Angelina the subjects of this, her most recent book, *The Invention of Wings*. In a blending of history and fiction, Kidd has created an extremely interesting tale which captivates and holds the reader throughout the book. Probably the earliest incident that foreshadows Sarah's behavior and sentiments throughout the story is her attempted refusal to accept the slave maid Handful as a gift from her father on her eleventh birthday.

Despite Sarah's protestations, Handful becomes her own personal serving maid, and eventually they become confidants as well as friends. Although Sarah cannot shield Handful from the punishments doled out to slaves, she secretly teaches her to read which was illegal and subject to severe penalties at that time. Their relationship is ambivalent, however. Handful is willful and resentful of her position and sometimes takes advantage of her mistress' leniency. This causes turmoil in the Grimke family who strongly believe that by law a slave is equivalent to 3/5 of a person and to educate him/her is treading on dangerous ground. In addition, Sarah commits the error of asserting her ambition to become a jurist someday like her father and brothers which appalls and shocks everyone. Since she is beginning to harbor intellectual pursuits inappropriate to a female, Sarah is not only banned from using her father's library but also relegated to the more feminine activities of needle-point and the like. Books and learning are Sarah's most precious and valued activities, and without them she falls into a deep depression. Read this wonderful account of the metamorphosis of this timid, stutter-prone young girl into one of the leading voices denouncing the evil of slavery. Sarah's closeness to Handful and dismay at what she witnesses the Negroes are made to endure is the impetus in Sarah's decision to do all in her power to effect their freedom. In this effort, she is joined by her younger sister Angelina. Kidd creates a fast-moving plot of slave rebellions and up-risings, dangerous attempts by runaways and insurgents to gain freedom, cruel and sadistic punishments when they are caught, and always the righteous wisdom and compassion of the main protagonist Sarah whose humanity cannot allow her to silently observe and do nothing. In my opinion, *The Invention of Wings* is superior in many respects to Kidd's *The Secret Life of Bees,* which was highly acclaimed and very popular.

MRS. GRANT AND MADAME JULE

by

Jennifer Chiaverini

Mrs. Grant and Madame Jule, as with Chiaverini's other works, *Mrs. Lincoln's Dressmaker* and *Mrs. Lincoln's Rival*, is historical fiction. Set in the mid-to-late 1800s, it not only provides background regarding the politics of the time, but also delves into the intriguing personalities of the primary characters and their relationships. The "Jule" in this story is the Negro slave given to Julia Grant by her father when she was four years-old. In childhood they were inseparable playmates, as close as sisters, but as they become older, their relationship becomes more ambivalent. When Julia marries the love of her life, Gen. Ulysses Grant, a Union soldier and ardent abolitionist, she still insists on keeping Jule who eventually runs away to freedom. Julia follows her husband wherever his battle missions take him, sometimes sleeping in tents in makeshift army camps. Even after four children, she continues to lend him the support of her presence, moving the entire family to towns and cities close to the battlefields. This is as much a love story as a war story. Her ardent devotion to him was the stuff of legends; his passionate love letters testimony to his overwhelming need for her.

The book is replete with information about historic Civil War battles -- Shiloh, Vicksburg, Appomattox -- as well as famous generals -- McClellan, Meade, Sherman, Sheridan, Ambrose Burnside, as well as the Confederate Robert E. Lee. But the strength of the author lies not in her research of these people and events (though it is thorough and accurate) but in her sharp portrayal of the characters who come alive through her writing.

Mary Todd Lincoln, for example, comes across as a mentally vulnerable, insecure, and troubled woman who takes offense easily and retains

grudges. Although a gracious hostess, she can be vindictive and superior, particularly with other women by whom she feels threatened. President Lincoln,
in contrast, is fair and just, humble and self-deprecating, devoted to his family,
as is General Grant, whom the President trusts completely to deliver the vic-
tories needed to end the war. Grant, himself, is totally dedicated to the cause,
devoted to his soldiers who are inspired by him, unpretentious, considerate
and empathetic, even of his enemies. A true gentleman of honor, integrity,
and humanity, Grant refuses to gloat over the fall of the South, and arranges
the surrender of Gen. Lee, in such a dignified manner so as to demonstrate the
utmost respect for his Southern counterpart. As for his wife Julia, she is an
adoring, admiring, unconditionally supportive wife and mother to their four
children, true to her marriage vow: "Wither thou goest, I will go." She wants
only to be with him, even when it requires extensive, uncomfortable, and dangerous travel; and she feels honored to be the wife of so fine a man. This is a
moving tale of the loving marriage of Julia and Ulysses Grant, our eighteenth
President, who shunned the limelight and felt more comfortable in the role of
soldier surrounded by his faithful troops than as Commander in Chief in the
White House. Still, when called to duty, whether in battle or government, he
never failed to respond, always with Julia by his side.

MRS. LINCOLN'S DRESSMAKER

by

Jennifer Chiaverini

Born into slavery, which was her life for thirty-seven years, Elizabeth Keckley purchased her freedom and that of her son Robert and moved to Washington, DC where she opened a dress shop. Through sheer tenacity, hard work, and an enterprising and entrepreneurial spirit, she honed her dressmaking skills to become the sole "modiste" and mantua maker of first, Mrs. Jefferson Davis; next, Mrs. Robert E. Lee; and eventually, Mary Todd Lincoln. For many years she was not only Mrs. Lincoln's personal assistant but also a close friend and confidant. As such, she was a close observer of not only the Lincoln family members but also history as it was enfolding throughout the Civil War years. She became a great admirer of Pres. Lincoln, who earned her respect by his devotion to his family and deep love for his children, by his humility and good-nature, by his integrity, and strength of character, his determination to hold the nation together, his total lack of ego, and his sincere sense of fairness and justice regarding the black race. She saw him weary from the stress of his office, heartbroken at the loss of young lives, burdened by the casualties and injuries suffered by those he had ordered into battle, and concerned and solicitous of his wife's fragile mental state. In all of this, she found it remarkable that Pres. Lincoln was able to maintain a sense of humor.

Having contacted a mild form of small pox and quarantined in the White House for three weeks, he joked weakly from his sickbed, "Now let the office seekers come, for at last I have something to give them." Her primary responsibility was to Mrs. Lincoln, not only in preparing her for state occasions, but more in tending to her changeable moods, calming her in her frequent anxiety attacks, bolstering her confidence, and advising her about her extravagant habits. It was only in Elizabeth that Mrs. Lincoln found solace and comfort and unconditional acceptance, devoid of criticism and judgment. Theirs was an unusual friendship -- black maid and First Lady -- and after her husband's assassination, Mary's dependence and need for Elizabeth was constant and unrelenting. After Mrs. Lincoln left the White House, she would summon Elizabeth to come tend to her in states far away -- New York, Illinois, etc. -- totally oblivious of the cost to Elizabeth personally or financially, since Elizabeth's business in Washington suffered from her many absences to respond to Mary's needs. Elizabeth never hesitated or refused. Despite this closest of bonds, their relationship was severed by what Mrs. Lincoln interpreted as a breach of confidence, although Elizabeth had never intended it to be so. This was truly tragic for both since Mrs. Lincoln ended up confined to an institution and Elizabeth in a home for destitute colored women.

Throughout the years Mrs. Lincoln refused to accept Elizabeth's many attempts to apologize and reconcile. It was a major loss for both of them since Elizabeth was the only one who had ever been able to soothe Mrs. Lincoln, and Elizabeth had sacrificed so much, including her own comfort and livelihood, to be at Mrs. Lincoln's side. This very good historical novel is worthwhile in two respects: it gives the reader further insight into two famous figures, Mr. and Mrs. Lincoln, and captures their feelings, as well as Elizabeth's point of view, regarding the events occurring during this time period.

I SHALL BE NEAR YOU

by

Erin Lindsay McCabe

I Shall Be Near You, set during the Civil War, is somewhat similar to a previous best-seller, *Cold Mountain,* in time, place, and characters. Both are love stories with a feisty female character, as well as chronicles of war. In this novel we have Rosetta, recently married to Jeremiah, who is intent on enlisting as a Union soldier not only to do his duty, but also to earn money with which he and Rosetta can buy their dream farm in Nebraska. Despite his reservations and reluctance, Rosetta convinces Jeremiah to allow her, disguised as a young boy, to accompany him. She is adamant in her refusal to remain safely at home. In fact, historical records indicate that there were at least two hundred women who joined their husbands to fight in this war. Rosetta is a combination of these female soldiers whom the author meticulously researched in preparation for writing this novel. Rosetta and Jeremiah's love is a sweet one that will be sorely tested as they face the dangers and horrors of battle, which McCabe describes in vivid detail and compelling prose. The narrative is told in first person from Rosetta's point of view in a realistic country dialect which rings with authenticity. In addition to creating this strong, complex female character, the author also provides accurate details regarding the battles of Bull Run and Antietam where the couple faces the Confederate Army in 1862. Prior to these battles, Rosetta decides to keep secret that she is pregnant, fearing discharge from the army and separation from Jeremiah who is also unaware of Rosetta's condition.

Much of the information contained in this book was gleaned from actual letters written by these women who served, particularly those by the real Sarah Rosetta Wakefield to her family back home. Another inspiration to the author was a New Jersey woman who in her second trimester was wounded, returned to duty, was promoted, fought in Fredericksburg in her third tri-mester, was promoted again, went into labor on picket duty, and delivered a baby boy, much to the surprise of her entire regiment. The Rosetta in this story is strong, plucky, determined, devoted to her spouse and cause, as were her real counterparts, heroines never mentioned in the history books. Erin McCabe has finally recognized them through *I Shall Be Near You*.

MARCH

by

Geraldine Brooks

For those who enjoyed reading about the March girls -- Jo, Meg, Beth, Amy and their mother Marmee -- in Louisa May Alcott's *Little Women* (1868), this recent book about their father's encounters while serving as a Civil War chaplain, might answer your questions about his absence in their lives. March, an ardent abolitionist who actually aided John Brown in securing arms for his attack on Harper's Ferry, sets out, zealous and idealistic, to be of aid to soldiers in the Union Army. Prior to his enlistment, he and his wife had assisted slaves seeking refuge in the North through the Underground Railroad. His initial intent had been to get a position in a church where he could decry from the pulpit " the barbarous system of slavery to all who would listen." There is a lot of historical detail here, regarding particular events as well as famous people -- Ralph Waldo Emerson, Henry Thoreau, Nathanial Hawthorne -- with whom the Marches are acquainted. Both moving and poignant, this is a tale of the horrors of war, of its traumatic effect on a decent and good man whose ideals are shattered by what he observes and experiences. In poetically descriptive prose, the author conveys an accurate picture of the war-ravaged South, its cotton plantations and mansions burned to the ground, its inhabitants, both black and white, the victims of immense fear and intense suffering. Vivid and wrenching is Brooks' description of the butchering not only on the battlefield, but also in the hastily erected hospital tents where March sees limbs amputated, shrapnel extracted from gangrenous wounds, young men blinded, crippled forever, howling in agony to the heavens. He will eventually return home, but physically and emotionally damaged, unhinged regarding his former moral certainties, guilt-ridden convinced that his own cowardice caused the death of those from whose aid he flinched. This is not only a well-wrought novel about the atrocities of war, but also the study of a man, his philosophy, his shortcomings, his sweet relationship with his daughters, his distancing from his wife and the eventual healing of their marriage. It can be considered "a sister work" to *Little Women*, but it can stand on its own as a first-rate novel. The historical research is considerable and the writing powerful, well-deserving of the Pulitzer Prize it was awarded.

THE HOUSE GIRL

by

Tara Conklin

Two remarkable heroines separated by a century: Josephine, a mulatto slave of a Southern plantation owner in the mid-1850s and Lina, a New York City lawyer assigned by her firm to research a reparations case on behalf of the descendants of Negro slaves.

The book's chapters alternate between the lives of the two women. Lina's assignment is to find a suitable plaintiff who legitimately represents the offspring of the thousands of blacks exploited for profit by their white owners. Her investigation leads her to the estate, now in ruins, of LuAnne Bell, an artist of some repute. As Lina becomes more enmeshed in the investigation, she is made aware that art connoisseurs have begun to question the identity of the paintings attributed to LuAnne Bell. All are unsigned, but on the back of each is written the name of the subject, each of whom had some familial attachment to the slave Josephine Bell, so named being the chattel of her mistress. Lina must make many trips to Lynnhurst, Virginia where the Bell Center for Women and Art stands on the property once owned by the Bells. Here, among the archives, she unearths the true story of Josephine and her sad and tragic life. Lina herself has a history of which she is only dimly aware. Abandoned at four years-old by her artist mother, she too has questions about her own past, which her father has chosen to remain undisclosed. This book is a search for the truth and the answers are not all happy ones. For a first novel, as well as a *New York Times* Bestseller, *The House Girl* is a credit to its author and the beginning of what I would expect to be a successful career as a writer.

A LAND REMEMBERED

by

Patrick Smith

A sweeping saga of an American frontier family, *A Land Remembered* traces the 1858 migration of Tobias McIvey, his wife Emma, and their infant son from poverty-stricken Georgia to the Florida wilderness. In a horse-drawn wagon they carried only seeds for planting, a shotgun, frying pan, cast iron pot, and tools. Their only means of sustenance were the berries Emma collected along the trail and the wild animals Tobias hunted. Life was primitive in the isolated scrub area where he erected a shaky lean-to.

They might not have survived their first year if not for the help and advice of some native Seminole Indians whom they befriended. Over the years this relationship would prove essential to Tobias, even saving his life. Theirs is a story of persistence and determination in the face of unrelenting heat, illness such as malaria and typhoid fever, near starvation, pestilence, drought, tempestuous storms, and every kind of natural disaster. In addition, their home would be burned and destroyed by Civil War soldiers and their cattle stolen by rustlers. But Tobias was not to be deterred on his quest for success and in Emma he had a willing and able partner. Their suffering and adversity was continuous, but it did not overwhelm them. Their very survival depended on their deep love and reliance on one another, as well as their tight bond of respect and devotion to mutual goals. The Florida landscape is as much an integral character in this book as Tobias, Emma, and their son Zech. The pages are lush with palm fronds, palmetto, cypress, hickory and giant oaks, tangled forests of impenetrable vines, low-lying river flats, muddy swamps and their predators -- bears, panthers, wolves, and rattlesnakes; it was kill or be killed. But there was serenity and unspoiled beauty as well -- snowy egrets, great-blue herons, whooping cranes, cormorants, and pink flamingos -- "their feathers catching the sunlight making them appear even pinker as they swoop over the shimmering surface of the water's edge, creating a sea of soft blue merging gently with clumps of willows and little islands of buttonbush with its creamy white flowers."

This is an exciting epic of adventure and romance; war and bloodshed; danger, hardship, pain and tragedy -- in which the McIvey's hardscrabble beginning will--in three generations -- culminate in the wealthy ownership of the most prized land in the development of Florida. The author, Patrick Smith, beautifully captures the essence of the land in its primitive state, long before it was found and settled -- when parts of it were Eden-like. He skillfully portrays men like Tobias and his Seminole comrades who cherished and respected their natural habitat and were willing to share its abundance before opportunistic and greedy developers raped its natural resources. The reader laments the arrival of the hucksters, real-estate entrepreneurs, and treasure seekers who, intent on making their fortunes, roamed from Tampa to Fort Pierce to Palm Beach to Miami with no concern for what they were destroying in their zeal for "progress."

The main character Tobias McIvey foreshadows this very reality when he says, "Perhaps animals are smarter than men, taking only what they need to live today, leaving something for tomorrow...Maybe it is man who will eventually perish as he destroys the land and all that it offers."

NB: Patrick Smith was nominated for the Pulitzer Prize for two previous novels: *Angel City* and *Forever Island.*

THE DARING LADIES OF LOWELL

by
Kate Alcott

The Daring Ladies of Lowell is set in Lowell and Fall River, Massachusetts where in the early 1830s many girls left their homes on rural farms to make new lives in these mill towns. Some were seeking to escape their confining and boring environments and domination by their fathers, others looking for independence and adventure. Such was the case for Alice Barrow and Lovey Cornell who became fast friends while working at a Lowell mill owned by the powerful and wealthy Fiske family. It was arduous and difficult labor under dangerous conditions, working from sunup to sunset on machinery in which hands and hair could easily be caught. In one instance, a girl's hair became entangled in a loom, lifting her off the factory floor, hanging for dear life until one of her agile co-workers cut her tresses, freeing her from the deadly grip of the machine. Another common and life-threatening hazard was inhalation of cotton which got into the lungs and caused pulmonary illness, choking all who eventually developed it. This was partly due to Hiram Fiske's refusal to open the windows, fearing that the air would dry out his precious cotton. His priority was profit, with no concern whatsoever for the health and welfare of those he was exploiting. Much to his dismay, his older son Samuel does not share his anti-humanitarian attitude and as the story progresses, actually defies his father. There is another younger brother Jonathan who is a lazy and irresponsible womanizer. The story becomes a mystery when Lovey is found dead and an autopsy reveals she was pregnant, much to Alice's astonishment. Disconsolate, she mourns the loss of her dearest friend and is adamant that the culprit be found.

Seeking to gain goodwill with the girls and diminish the unrest about working conditions that has been brewing among his employees, Hiram Fiske puts all his efforts into seeking and trying to indict Lovey's assaulter.

The two best features of the plot are the escalating tension of the trial and the budding relationship between Samuel Fiske and Alice. Another most intriguing character is the Rev. Ephraim Avery, a preacher then well-known in the Fall River area. *The Daring Ladies of Lowell* is a skillful blend of mystery and romance.

ORPHAN TRAIN

by

Christina Baker Kline

In our US history texts, there is little mention of some past events with which our country is uncomfortable, such as the internment of Japanese-Americans in camps in California following the bombing of Pearl Harbor during WWII. Due to national hysteria regarding Asians, the homes, businesses, and property of these loyal citizens, some of whom had family members serving in the US military, were confiscated. Their lives were disrupted and changed forever as they were forced to take up residence in ramshackle barracks. When allowed to return to their homes after the war, they found their businesses had become worthless and their property often inhabited by strangers. *Orphan Train* tells of another blight on the landscape of American history -- that of the transport of more than 250,000 orphaned and neglected children from East Coast cities to farmlands in the Midwest between 1859 and 1929. It was the intent of The Children's Aid Society to place these children in homes in Minnesota, Kansas, and Iowa with families who would raise them to become educated, independent, moral, hard-working Christians. In reality little oversight existed once the children were left in these bleak, isolated prairie towns where many became little more than indentured, abused, overworked servants. So begins the story of Vivian Daly, nee Niamh Power, an Irish immigrant who, at age seven, loses all of her family in a devastating fire. On the train west, she meets a young boy named Duchy, who is much more aware of what awaits them than she, and like Vivian, has no control over his fate. This is a moving and wrenching story of survival and endurance in which Vivian must adjust and adapt to hardship, loneliness, and subjugation of not only her past, but also her feelings. In each family with which she is placed, she becomes a victim again and again, resented and mistrusted by those who consider her a foreigner and outsider. Totally unloved and friendless, she fortunately encounters a kindly schoolteacher and her compassionate landlady who find a suitable older couple, the Dalys, to adopt her. Despite their devotion to her, Vivian still finds it difficult to emotionally connect -- possibly because she has had to suppress her emotions so deeply. Eventually she is reunited with Duchy, but it ends tragically. There are three parts to this story: Vivian's early life in the Midwest; her adoption by Mr. and Mrs. Daly, as well as her reunion with Duchy; and her life as an elderly woman when, at ninety-one she becomes acquainted with Molly, a troubled teen whose community service substitute for probation places her with Vivian. This last segment is actually the most interesting since parts of Vivian's past, which she has kept secret from everyone, are revealed with the assistance of Molly.

STELLA BAIN

by

Anita Shreve

1916. World War I. An American female ambulance driver awakens in an army field hospital tent for the wounded in France. She has suffered a concussion, resulting in the total loss of memory. When asked her name, she hesitates and finally replies Stella Bain although she is not sure why she chooses it. She herself wonders who is Stella Bain and what is her past. She only knows that she is experiencing an urgent need to find the British Admiralty Building in London where she senses there might be a clue to her real identity. Upon her arrival in England, she becomes very ill and collapses in front of the home of Lily Bridge and her husband August, who is a psychiatrist. Through talk therapy and her artistic drawings, Dr. Bridge attempts to assist her in finding answers to her past. After five trips together to the British Admiralty headquarters, a stranger recognizes her and addresses her as Edna Bliss. Almost instantly she remembers that she has children somewhere. So begins an arduous journey to unearth the facts and find her family. There will be a number of shocking surprises: an aborted love affair; an abusive husband; trauma from the observation of the most horrendous war injuries; an extremely close emotional relationship with one of the injured and disfigured soldiers Philip who has lost half of his face on the battlefield; an attempt to set right a wrong for which she feels responsible; dealing with guilt from her abandonment of her children; and the understanding of the results of post-traumatic stress disorder, for which there was no treatment and of which there was little knowledge at that time. This is a novel of resilience, the healing of physical and emotional wounds, and eventual rebirth.

Anita Shreve is a well-known author with sixteen previous and popular books to her credit. In this her most recent, she relies to a great extent on coincidence since Philip, the injured soldier, is the brother of Edna's previous fiancé who spurned her for another years ago. Nevertheless, Shreve has created a plot that holds the reader's interest; and for those who are romantically inclined, an ending in which Edna finds love once again.

GIRL IN THE BLUE DRESS:
A NOVEL INSPIRED BY THE LIFE
& MARRIAGE OF CHARLES DICKENS

by

Gaynor Arnold

An outstanding work, *Girl in the Blue Dress* is based on the marriage of Catherine and Charles Dickens, who was the pre-eminent writer of the Victorian Age, although in this book they are named Dorothea and Alfred Gibson. It is not only the story of their young romance and courtship when Catherine fell wildly in love and under the spell of this hypnotic and mesmerizing figure, but also a psychological analysis of personality traits influencing the relationship between a flamboyant, restless man bent on personal and financial success and his adoring, but insecure wife. Dickens had suffered an unstable childhood plagued by poverty, separated at twelve years-old from his family when they were housed in Debtors' Prison (London) for non-payment of debts. Before their imprisonment, Charles' mother had found him a job pasting labels on bottles in a blacking warehouse among ignorant and illiterate hoodlums and riffraff. Denied the education he so sorely craved, this experience so shamed and embarrassed him that even years later when he was an acclaimed author, he could never bring himself to walk past that building he so loathed.

Carrying these emotional scars throughout his entire life, he drove himself mercilessly to earn money through his writings, often laboring at his desk both day and night until he collapsed from exhaustion. His marriage suffered not only from his workaholic nature, but also from Catherine's numerous pregnancies (ten in all, losing two children) which left her depleted and depressed. In an effort to assist Catherine in the running of such a large household, her younger sister "Alice" was invited to live with the Dickens' brood. Her presence changed the family dynamics, as she became both substitute mother and pseudo-wife. Sister-in-law and brother-in-law became so close that when she died unexpectedly at twenty five, Charles was disconsolate and drifted into an emotionally paralyzed state.

Hysterical over her passing, he removed a ring from her finger and wore it the rest of his life, as well as requesting to someday be buried with her.

Catherine and Charles drifted even further apart, when he sent her to recuperate at a sanitarium and "Sissy," another of Catherine's sisters came to take over the household. This arrangement eventually led first to "Sissy" displacing Catherine as woman of the house, and later to Catherine's eventual banishment to a small, shabby residence, isolated from her children who were discouraged from communicating with their mother.

For years I have been an ardent fan of Charles Dickens, undoubtedly a literary genius. The first chapter of his novel *Great Expectations* is considered by critics to be the most finely crafted opening chapter in all of English literature. I have literally cried over the fate of his tragic characters (Pip, Oliver Twist, David Copperfield, etc. and been held in taut suspense by his intricately woven plots, the end of each chapter a cliff-hanger. He actually serialized his novels -- publishing a chapter bi- monthly in a magazine so that his avid reading audience waited hungrily for the next installment. Immensely popular in both Great Britain and America, he was considered a man of fine character -- a family man -- who focused attention on the plight of the impoverished, particularly orphaned street urchins and neglected children. But the cruel and shabby treatment of the wife who was so devoted to him and loved him beyond measure, revealed a disturbing side of Dickens' nature. This is the same man whose heart-rending descriptions of the trials and tribulations of the powerless evoke such sympathy as to make the reader's heart ache.

This is the story of a woman married to a rising star, who with each success leaves her farther and farther behind. It is a story of a gifted but complex man, a sort of compartmentalized "Jekyll and Hyde," who strives all his life for fame and fortune which unfortunately and ultimately consume him. Moreover, it is the sad tale of the breakdown of a once loving marriage.

THE DRESSMAKER'S WAR

by

Mary Chamberlain

Set in World War II, this work of historical fiction is the poignant, harrowing tale of Ada Vaughan, a talented British seamstress who has the misfortune of meeting and falling for a con artist, Stanislaus von Lieben who convinces her to follow him to Paris. After a brief love affair, he abandons her there just as the city is invaded by Germany. Unaware that she is already pregnant, Ada seeks refuge in a convent of nuns with whom she works nursing the sick and elderly under the guise of Sister Clara. There she encounters an elite elderly German, Professor Weiss, who is attracted to her and often summons her to keep him company in the private conservatory. Soon with the help of the sisters, she gives birth to a baby she names Thomas who is immediately surrendered to an elderly priest in hopes of finding a safe home for the infant. Overcome with an overwhelming sense of loss and anxiety for her child, Ada becomes first hysterical, then lethargic and profoundly depressed. When Herr Weiss summons her again, she is so emaciated and hopeless that her actions have become robotic. Now he demands much more than conversation and she has no choice but to acquiesce. Once it becomes known that she is a very skilled dressmaker, it appears that she might escape his assaults when she is placed in the home of the commandant of the Dachau concentration camp. Although locked in a room, fed only scraps, overworked and beaten by the mistress of the house, she is able to find purpose and protection in creating fashionable dresses for the German ladies, friends of the mistress. There are a number of equally gripping chapters which the author makes of Ada's life: her bleak and tortured existence as a Nazi prisoner and her return to England, free but broken in body and spirit. Your heart aches for this helpless victim of misplaced love in a man she trusted; of a mother's constant agonized yearning and frantic search for her child; for her misery and horrific experiences of war;

and finally for her unfair, misogynist prosecution in a British court of law. Her ability to survive and endure such brutality and personal devastation makes for a thrilling, but haunting story. A well-rendered female protagonist, Ada Vaughn actually lives on the pages of this book and will linger with you long after you have finished her story.

THE BOOK OF ARON

by

Jim Shepard

Mesmerizing! Heart-breaking! Shocking! Such is the tale told by a young Jewish boy named Aron caught up in the nightmare of war in Poland. He starts out as a naive 9 year-old with little self-confidence, beset upon and criticized by his siblings for his ineptitude at everything he attempts. He is often beaten by his father for failing to understand the most basic instructions and commands, and finds solace only in the protection of his mother who seems to comprehend and accept his limitations. But Aron learns that he is good at something essential. When his family is starving, he is the one who is able to smuggle food due to his cleverness as well as his diminutive size and quick legs. It is dangerous -- actually life-threatening -- since such thieves are summarily executed by the Gestapo which the boy has witnessed firsthand. Not only must he outwit the German officers, but also the thuggish gangs who are as desperate as he and as brutal as the enemy. Through the child's words and eyes, the reader becomes acutely cognizant of the haunting terror, sorrowful anguish, gnawing hunger, frigid and numbing cold, and devastating loss that Aron suffers daily. When his entire family is transported by train to the death camps, he barely survives on the street, escaping capture before he is rescued by Janusz Korczak, the famous doctor who was put in charge of the Warsaw orphanage during WWII. But life in this institution is hell -- children die every day of typhus, tuberculosis, dehydration, pneumonia, malnutrition, infection. Even those who barely survive are plagued with lice, hunger, dysentery, depression, inertia, shock, trauma, and abysmal unsanitary conditions.

Illness and disease are rampant and the details of what Aron describes are appalling -- the suffering unendurable to these most innocent victims. This book is not for the faint-of-heart. All of us are aware of the savagery, brutality, and inhumanity of Germany's attempt to annihilate the Jewish population in

Europe; but this first-hand account, narrated in a child's simple language -- a child who cannot possibly comprehend the dire events that engulf and imprison him -- arouses the reader's compassion, horror, and outrage simultaneously.

GIRL AT WAR

by
Sara Novic

Remarkable for a debut novel! Novic is an extremely talented new author who, against the background of the Yugoslavian Civil War of the 1990s, weaves a mesmerizing tale. The main character Ana lives with her parents and baby sister Rahela in a small apartment in Croatia's capital. As they go about their daily life, Ana senses the increasing anxiety hovering around her family as Serbian forces approach their area. Other families are leaving, but life continues for Ana, a tomboy who spends much of her time with a neighbor boy Luka, playing games, riding bikes. Soon the war encroaches upon them, making necessary midnight trips to the shelters as bombs explode around their homes. Procuring food becomes more and more difficult, and the situation is made worse by the fact that baby Rahela is wasting away, crying in pain for days from a combination of hunger and some undiagnosed illness. Finally, Ana's mother insists that they take a trip by car across the border to a medical mission run by American doctors in Slovenia. There they learn that Rahela is extremely ill and her kidneys are shutting down. Their only hope is to send her to the US for treatment, but she must be taken there by an American doctor and placed with a foster family. The parents are distraught, never expecting this outcome; and for the first time, Ana sees her father sob, overwhelmed by the imminent loss of his child and the deteriorating situation in Croatia. On their way home, the family is stopped by enemy Serbs, made to abandon their car, and forced to a previously dug, make-shift grave with other prisoners, who are being shot in sequence around the oval pit. As the gunmen make their way around the circle toward Ana and her family, her father maintains the presence of mind to whisper instructions in her ear. What follows is horror unimaginable. This is the beginning of an amazing odyssey which the author describes in tightly woven scenes, suspenseful and nightmarish causing both physical and emotional scars from the trauma. This is a heart-rending account of one girl's inability to bury the past -- she cannot forget what she has lost and the pain and agony she has suffered.

I have visited Croatia (previously known as Yugoslavia following the civil conflicts in the 1990s. In addition, I have been to Slovenia more recently. Croatia has been rebuilt and its scenic beauty is impressive, particularly the rugged coastline splendor on the Adriatic side. On my first trip, I was vaguely aware of its tragic past. But this book, more than any news story or TV coverage, simultaneously enlightened and horrified me as to the extent of man's inhumanity to man in this otherwise peaceful and beautiful location.

NECESSARY LIES

by

Diane Chamberlain

Necessary Lies is a most sensitive portrayal of the plight of poor, rural tenant farmers in North Carolina in the 1960s. The main characters are 15 year-old Ivy, subject to epileptic seizures; her older sister Mary Ella, an unmar-ried teenage mother; and Jane Forrester, the newly-hired, inexperienced so-cial worker assigned to the Hart family. There is much conflict, both internal and external, in this novel, which the author does a marvelous job in develop-ing. First is the tension between Jane and her new husband Robert, a pediatri-cian, whose masculine ego is threatened by his wife's desire to work outside the home. Then there are the chronic disagreements Jane encounters with her supervisors at the Department of Public Health regarding her interaction as a social worker with her clients, particularly the Hart family and another headed by a black matriarch named Lita Jordan. The main criticism is that Jane "cares too much," becomes too involved with some in her caseload. Both Hart and Jordan families live on property owned by Mr. Gardiner who at first appears to be a sort of benevolent overseer. Secrets abound in the experiences of these characters who are reticent and guarded, knowing their lives are entirely controlled by both the welfare department and Mr. Gardiner, who on a mo-ment's whim can turn them out of their homes. Theirs is a compelling and cap-tivating story that will tug at your heartstrings and prick your sense of justice. You will cheer-on the kind-hearted and compassionate Jane who will repeat-edly rebel against the outmoded and autocratic rules of a welfare system that thinks in statistics and "fixing" social problems without consideration of the very people whose lives they are supposed to be improving. Chamberlain, the author, will deal with moral issues -- incest, teen pregnancy, dependence on the welfare system, exploitation, and forced sterilization -- which was actually practiced until 1974 by the state of North Carolina under the direction of The

Eugenics Board. Your heart will ache for the unknowing victims who have no voice or power even over their own lives and bodies. Does poverty and the need for public assistance negate all personal rights? In this novel, the dialogue of the characters, particularly that of Ivey, is eloquent even in its uneducated, Southern country dialect as she demonstrates such love for her family, her unborn child, and a deep understanding of right and wrong despite unreliable IQ tests and hasty, shoddy medical examinations that "label" her of low intelligence. Chamberlain so deftly demonstrates that there is nothing "low" about Ivey Hart, that she is in every way a responsible, smart, ambitious, hardworking young woman with dreams of her own. The book builds to its suspenseful conclusion with both Ivey and her advocate Jane about to testify at a hearing in 2011 brought by the North Carolina Justice for Sterilization Victims Foundation, which actually occurred. *Necessary Lives* ever so smoothly interweaves history with fiction and results in the reader becoming emotionally involved with its two feisty and determined heroines, Ivey and Jane, who inspire the reader's admiration. The book leaves you with the question: What might have been the fate of so many more like Ivey and her mentally ill sister Mary Ella if not for the concern and intercession of the Jane Forresters who rebelled against their ill treatment and abuse and advocated for fairer and more humane practices in dealing with such "problematic" families?

THE MAGIC STRINGS OF FRANKIE PRESTO

by

Mitch Albom

If you are a music enthusiast familiar with tunes and artists from the 1950s, '60s, '70s, you might enjoy this somewhat unusual book.

First of all, it is an epic tale of an extremely talented guitarist, Frankie Presto, whose story is narrated by "Music," which for the purposes of this book, is personified. Told from the omniscient point of view, "Music" has been a gift bestowed upon Frankie at birth when his mother delivered him in a church during the Spanish Civil War. As his mother lay dying, the nun who assisted with Frankie's birth, flees with him. Eventually he will be raised in an orphanage before being adopted by "Baffa" who, recognizing the boy's musical nature, sends him for lessons with "Maestro," a blind master of the guitar. This instructor will be a demanding taskmaster, not only honing Frankie's incredible musical ability but also guiding him in the ways of life. "Everyone joins a band in this life," he tells Frankie. "Only some of them play music." Of course, what Maestro means is that the family unit is the first "band" in which we all play followed by other bands of which we become members -- friendship, romance, school, neighborhoods, army, work -- in which each of us plays a part. I very much like the author's clever use of musical imagery as he develops the various parts of Frankie's life. For example, when Frankie falls in love and marries, the author describes it in musical terms. "Since all love stories are symphonies ... they have four movements. First there is *allegro*, the quick and spirited opening of any relationship, followed by *adagio*, a slow turn. Then *minuet/scherzo*, short steps in 3/4 time, and lastly *rondo*, a repeating theme, interrupted by various passages." Using these categories, Albom will continue to tell of the various ups and downs of Frankie's marriage and musical career. (Again the mantra "Everyone joins a band in life; sometimes it's the wrong one.") And what a career it is! The author flashes back in each chapter to some

111

person who has been influenced or impressed by Frankie and his music. Burt Bacharach will talk of hearing Frankie from an adjacent booth in a recording studio. Hank Williams, a country star, meets Frankie in a music store. Darlene Love sees him at The Hollywood Bowl opening for Nat King Cole. Frank Sinatra and Bobby Darin recall their friendship with him, as do Dizzy Gillespie, the famous jazz trumpeter, Louis Armstrong, Duke Ellington, James Brown, Chubby Checker, Chuck Berry, Little Richard, the Everly Brothers, Carly Simon, David Bowie, Barbara Streisand, and other great artists in the music industry. Always in the background are the tunes which will resonate with people of my generation: "Will You Still Love Me Tomorrow?" "Bill Bailey Won't You Please Come Home?" and "All I Have to Do Is Dream," to name just a few.

From the beginning to the end of the book is an element of mystery, even a sense of eeriness as there is a "presence" or spirit always hovering in the shadows as if watching and waiting -- even protecting Frankie as he veers off course. Another feature I liked was the realistic conversational dialect of the musicians, many black, who comment on their interactions with Frankie. It adds an element of local color. This is not your ordinary read. Albom's inventiveness and imagination are at work here, creating a mystical aura to it all.

THE SWANS OF FIFTH AVENUE

by

Melanie Benjamin

The Swans of Fifth Avenue focuses on the unique and unusual relationship between five ultra-glamorous, ultra-wealthy, ultra-chic women and their literary genius friend Truman Capote, author of "Best-selling" works *Breakfast at Tiffanys, In Cold Blood,* and others. Truman grew up a needy and insecure child partly due to his parents' rejection of him so that he craved love and attention all his adult life. These six women -- socialites who were the epitome of beauty and elegance -- namely, CZ Guest, Gloria Guinness, Slim Keith, Pamela Churchill Harriman, Marella Agnelli, and in particular the -- one and only Babe Paley -- welcomed him into their private circle and provided him with acceptance and support (both emotional and financial) for the many years of their friendship. In return, he entertained them with the most delicious gossip, outrageous stories, shocking and titillating anecdotes -- the life of every party they gave, the center of their attention. Through them he gained access to their powerful and influential husbands and friends, as well as their magnificent estates and villas, luxurious 5th Avenue penthouses, Mediterranean cruising yachts where he was often their guest. This was a reciprocal arrangement. Whether intentionally or not, they used him to amuse them, to distract them from any unpleasantness in their lives; and he used them to compensate for his loneliness and ostracism for homosexuality. Truman was a strange creature indeed -- besides his pudgy baby face, pale coloring, and thin, wispy blond hair, he wore velvet jackets and long trailing scarves. At times he was resentful, often feeling he was merely their "boy toy," a type of jester who had always to sparkle and shine and mesmerize them with his vibrancy. But they really did "adore" him, no one less than the most exquisite of all -- Babe Paley, wife of the powerful head of CBS, Bill Paley. It was with Truman that Babe felt comfortable enough to confide her innermost fears, disappointments, sadness and loneliness. Only with him could she be honest, free of subterfuge and artifice, and to him she bared her soul. Lest you dismiss this story as a tale of superficial, vacant, condescending women -- although that depicts much of their behavior -- I should point out that there is deep portrayal of character here. The author, Melanie Benjamin, is adept at capturing the essence of the intimate relationship between Babe and Truman. She is masterful at allowing us a peek into their close interaction. One particularly poignant scene has Babe allowing Truman -- only Truman -- to slowly, gently, lovingly remove all the heavy make-up she employs to camouflage the scars of an early car accident. She has never allowed anyone to see the real face -- not even her husband who has never seen her without the make-up and painful false teeth she wears even to bed because her mother had reminded her again and again that her "face was her ticket" to a "good marriage." As he reveals her face with all its "imperfections," Truman declares her "beautiful. I don't see scars. I see you. Perfect. I love you for who you are, not what you look like" -- which he sincerely means. She needs no mask with him. In another equally touching scene, she asks him to keep her company throughout the night -- to allay her aching need for companionship -- and they sleep together chastely in her bed simply holding hands. He knew her better than her own husband and Truman hated Bill for neglecting and hurting her with his disregard and infidelities. Truman was her "friend, her heart, her soul, her confidant." Yes, there are adulterous affairs in this book, bad behavior, emphasis on material possessions, eliteness, prestige and social connections; but there is substance in the relationship between two very damaged, lonely souls who feel a kinship from the moment they meet. "What is your greatest fear?" Truman asks Babe. "That someone will see. That someone will find me out... and that no one will love me truly." In Truman she finds unconditional love. And with her he too shares secrets, hopes, and dreams. The author does a fine job of portraying the many faceted Babe as a sympathetic character -- the victim of social-climbing parents; an abused, under-appreciated and long-suffering wife yearning for love in a loveless marriage; a true and loyal friend; a courageous woman facing illness. Read this very spellbinding book to learn about the ultimate betrayal that changes everything.

NON-FICTION

DEAD WAKE:
THE LAST CROSSING OF THE LUSITANIA

by

Erik Larson

On May 1, 1915 the fastest and most luxuriously appointed ship of that time, the *Lusitania* set sail from New York bound for Liverpool, England with 1959 persons aboard, including crew and passengers. *Dead Wake* is the compelling story of its last trans-Atlantic crossing. Erik Larson has woven history with narrative to create a book that reads more like an engrossing novel, complete with mystery, suspense, drama, intrigue, warfare, and disaster. In the opening chapters we are introduced to the various travelers as well as the captain himself, William Thomas Turner, the most experienced and well-respected of the Cunard Co. of large sea vessels. Although Germany and Great Britain were engaged in war, the United States remained neutral under the leadership of Pres. Woodrow Wilson; and despite a warning issued by Germany stating its intention to attack any ships passing through "patrol-zone" waters, no one believed that one carrying civilians was in any danger. As a result, those on board the *Lusitania* engaged in leisure pursuits -- playing cards, reading, drinking, smoking, dining, walking on deck, playing shuffle-board -- oblivious to the danger that awaited them. Through detailed description of the dress, activities, and conversations of the various travelers, Larson provides us with an almost visual picture of these days sailing the Atlantic, successfully capturing a time and place. The reader can imagine the nannies pushing the infant passengers in their prams, the toddlers chasing each other around the decks, children jump-roping -- since there were ninety-five children and thirty-nine babies traveling with parents. Ironically, a family with the last name of Luck -- a mother and her two children -- were going to England to be reunited with the father. Unfortunately, that would not happen. As the reader becomes acquainted with the various travelers and the reasons for their travel to England on this ship, they become "real" to us -- not as characters in a book, but as living persons, which indeed they were. And so, their terrible fate becomes all the more horrible when, on an otherwise tranquil, calm and balmy spring day, the ship is torpedoed by a German U-boat and sinks within eighteen minutes. The scenes of chaos that ensue -- the frantic and unsuccessful attempts to lower lifeboats (only six of twenty-two; the confusion of passengers, many of whom don life-preservers upside down; the separation of mothers from their children, husbands from their wives, create a scenario similar to what occurred on the *Titanic.* Just as in the case of this earlier disaster, it was believed that the *Lusitania* was too big, too well-built and too fast to be sunk. The author skillfully creates suspense even before the actual attack occurs, as he depicts the character of the German submarine commander Walther Schweiger who, like a predator, is lying in wait for his unsuspecting victim. Larson conveys Schweiger's mounting frustration as he is thwarted repeatedly by fog, fear of discovery, inability to communicate with head- quarters, and extremely stifling and uncomfortable conditions within the submarine. This makes for extreme tension. In addition, the description of the aftermath is both horrifying and mesmerizing -- the swell of geysers spouting violently from the combustion, the positions of victims dangling from the ship or leaping across wide open space to jump into lifeboats, bodies in the most grotesque positions attached to life-jackets bobbing in the ocean, hundreds of waving hands desperately reaching out above the sea just before drowning. This book reads like a thriller with strong emotional impact. In addition to the intriguing plot is an analysis of "what-ifs" -- what if the *Lusitania's* departure had not been delayed in NY as it was by taking on additional passengers from another ship; what if Captain Turner had been running it on all four engines rather than three because fuel was being rationed during war time; what if the early morning fog had not lifted allowing the German captain clear visibility and aim at his target. The final chapter delves into the British Admiralty's attempt to use the Captain as a scapegoat for this disaster despite the fact that they had not shared with him essential knowledge of which they were aware. This is one compelling story that will stay with you long after you have completed the reading.

EMPTY MANSIONS

by

Bill Dedman and Paul Clark Newell, Jr.

Fascinating! Unusual! Mysterious! Engrossing! Such is the tale of Huguette Clark, daughter of W. A. Clark, a self-made copper industrialist, railroad baron, and founder of Las Vegas. Born in a log cabin in Pennsylvania in 1839, W.A. began as a prospector for gold in Montana and through sheer grit and ingenuity, amassed a fortune rivaling, and possibly surpassing, oilman J.D. Rockefeller in the 1900s. In that time, he was often referred to as the "incredible" copper king. When he died in 1925, he left an estate estimated at $100 million to $250 million, worth up to $3.4 billion today. In 1895 he built a one hundred and twenty one room, Beaux Arts mansion, on Fifth Avenue up the street from Vanderbilt and Astor, down from Andrew Carnegie. When completed, this house was called "the most remarkable dwelling in the world... without doubt the most costly and most beautiful private residence in America." There were exquisite classical carvings, gilded panels obtained from Paris, marble columns, a clock from the boudoir of Marie Antionette, a tower one hundred feet above the street -- even a quarantine suite in case of a pandemic. These were the opulent quarters in which his daughters Andree and Huguette resided. Not only is the story of W. A.'s seeking his fortune in the Wild West truly awe-inspiring -- he was an intrepid and ingenious force with which to be reckoned -- but also intriguing is the life of his daughter Huguette, who after her sister's death at sixteen, became his heir. Huguette was a shy and reticent girl, uncomfortable in the limelight, shunning publicity all her life. The most intriguing part of this story is what became of her in her adulthood. Guarded and reclusive, she spent all of her time in her palatial apartments, refusing nearly all human contact. Even her trusted financial advisors had never actually seen her, communicating only by letter, telegram, phone, or through a door. All but her trusted caretakers, considered her eccentric. For one thing, she collected dolls throughout her entire life, well into her nineties. She commissioned Dior to design the latest Paris fashions for them and placed them in doll houses she had personally designed and ordered from her personal cabinetmaker in France. She actually played with them, dressing and undressing them, moving them around for various activities -- tea parties, walking in the garden, having conversations. In one instance, she had the cabinetmaker remake the doll house since the ceilings were too low, and as she wrote to him, "The little people are banging their heads." She collected all sorts of dolls, American Barbies with all the furniture and accessories, and historic Japanese "hina-ningo." In the design of the houses, she would instruct the maker about where to place windows and doors and how they should open, how to design the staircases, specified the measurements down to a quarter inch; she possessed an artistic sensibility, imagination, and meticulous drive for precision. Lest the reader dismiss her as "crazy," many caretakers, as well as those with whom she communicated by phone or pen, unanimously described her as polite, delightful, animated, sweet, happy, lucid, and extremely magnanimous. Generously, she gave huge sums of money as gifts to those closest to her -- particularly her caretaker, Hadassah Peri, on whom she was dependent for much of her later life. She had a kind heart and would give and sell valuable paintings by Monet, Degas, and Renoir, as well as Cartier and Tiffany jewels, to aid those she felt in need, when toward the end of her life she had given so much cash away, that selling possessions became necessary. The last twenty years of her life were spent cocooned in a room at Doctors' Hospital, Beth Israel despite the fact that she was not physically ill. She had been admitted for treatment of facial cancers but decided to remain there for the rest of her life. When her distant family members became suspicious that she might be under the influence of her caretaker and attorneys, they attempted to intervene, but were quickly rebuffed. Was she just a uniquely unusual, independent, munificent, private soul or was she manipulated by greedy friends and advisors intent on self-aggrandizement? This question is never resolved and the reader must decide for himself. The book is well-researched, well-documented, and well-written. In the end, she may have just been a willful, shrewd, stubborn, extremely wealthy woman who chose to live her life on her own terms, using her money to reward those who enabled her to live in privacy and seclusion, which was her primary wish.

BORN ROUND

by
Frank Bruni

"Born round, you don't die square"
(Frank Bruni's grandmother)

Frank Bruni, former restaurant critic for *The New York Times*, has written a candid biography of his lifelong struggles with food -- overeating, purging, using diets and diet pills, trying all types of exercise regimens, as well as suffering from bulimia. Growing up in an Italian family, he consumed second, third and fourth helpings as far back as he could remember. To refuse the fried dough (fritte) his grandmother offered him was the "equivalent of turning his face away when she went to kiss him." His mother also equated food with love. In addition, she could not imagine how other families managed without a freezer and second refrigerator in the garage, despite a large Sub-Zero in the kitchen. Of his parents, he says, "Mom and Dad bought enough food for a small country; Liechtenstein, for sure." When his parents bought a home in California, they were delighted that in their kitchen was a center island with an old-fashioned soda fountain with bays and spigots for different syrups, a wand that produced carbonated water, and deep compartments for huge tubs of ice cream -- three different flavors -- which they lugged home in huge cylindrical columns from Baskin Robins to lower into this treasured gadget. Moreover, he recalls Thanksgivings when his mom roasted a number of turkey breasts, in addition to the main bird, because it would be unthinkable to not have enough left over for late night snacks or lunch the following day. As a result, he developed a "McMansion of a stomach," and an unhealthy relationship with food. He ate to steady his nerves, alleviate anxiety, ease loneliness, and substitute boredom. At some point, however, he realized he could no longer blame his weight problems on his family's conditioning or his current job which, at his lowest point, was as a political correspondent on the George W. Bush campaign. The plane travel, rushed pace, and late night hours allowed no time for exercise and plenty of junk food and alcohol. The nadir comes when he offers a friend a ride home in his car, and she must gingerly side step the mounds of bones on the floor. Mortified, he realizes they are the remains of the take-out Chinese chicken wings from the night before when he was so ravenous, he gluttonously devoured them while driving home. Food had become his enemy by his gross over-indulgence and threatened his health, his personal relationships, and even his self- respect. Read to find out how he eventually succeeds in overcoming his excesses, curbing his appetite so that he is able to appreciate quality rather than quantity.

THE 50 GREATEST LOVE LETTERS OF ALL TIME

Edited by
David H. Lowenherz

From the Australian writer Katherine Mansfield's (1885-1923) passionate and highly sensual declaration of love to the more mundane and succinct "I'm sure crazy to see you" Harry Truman (1884-1972) to his adored wife Bess, this book is a collection of some of the most highly charged and emotional personal expressions of romantic love expressed by smitten individuals through the centuries. These epistolary compositions are not only impressive in the depth and degree of ardor they convey, but also provide us with a glimpse into the personality of the writer himself/herself. Some lines border on high poetry, as in Oscar Wilde's letter to his wife Constance: "My soul and body are mingled in some exquisite ecstasy with yours;" while others profess a transcendent love that knows no earthly bounds, as in Civil War General George Custer's (1839-1876) letter to his wife Elizabeth: "With thoughts of my darling my last prayer will be for her, my last breath will speak her name." In fact, Custer risked everything he had worked so hard to achieve when he made an unauthorized visit to Elizabeth at a nearby fort during a frontier mission against the Sioux and Cheyenne Indians. As a result, he was court-martialed and suspended for a year. Her devotion to him was legendary, following him everywhere he was stationed, sacrificing her own comfort and security to accompany him. One interesting inclusion was a letter to Elvis Presley from an admiring fan Marjorie Fossa after seeing him in concert in 1972; it is less poetic than the others but certainly no less sincere. She tells him she has worked three jobs throughout her school years in order to purchase "all of his music and ANYTHING else" that she could get her hands on. She declares that seeing him on stage was "the most exciting day of my life (more so than my wedding day!)"

She actually was fired from her job after she took the day off for the concert, but she adds in the letter, "I am now on cloud 9,000 ... it was worth losing fifty jobs." From Abigail Adams to Honore de Balzac to Frida Kahlo to Dylan Thomas to Virginia Woolf's "It is incredible how essential to me you have become," all express the same sentiments albeit in the different phrasing of each individual: that the object of their affection is the dearest, most precious, most treasured person in their lives upon whom their happiness depends. It will restore your belief in the possibility and existence of TRUE LOVE.

LIAR, TEMPTRESS, SOLDIER, SPY

by
Karen Abbott

What an interesting telling of history! Kate Abbott has meticulously researched and chronicled the lives of four truly remarkable females who risked everything for their political cause during the Civil War. Belle Boyd and Rose O'Neal Greenhow worked in support of the Confederacy, while Elizabeth Van Lew and Emma Edmonds were on the Union side. All were strong, courageous, daring and defiant -- valuable assets to their respective governments. Belle Boyd was probably the most daring of all. A skilled equestrian and marksman, at seventeen she became a "Rebel" who felt it her duty to entrap Yankee officers, using her guiles and beauty to extract information about troop numbers, their movements, as well as the state of their army's morale. All this was fed to Stonewall Jackson, the leading general of the Confederate Army. She idolized him despite his peculiarities: odd flip-flop boots hanging on size fourteen feet; his horse "Fancy" only fifteen hands high so that Jackson had to ride him with his feet drawn up so as to avoid dragging them on the ground. In addition, he believed himself to be "out of balance" so that even under fire in battle, he would stop, raise one arm waiting for the blood to rush down his body to establish equilibrium. Belle was no "wilting violet" and actually shot at point blank a Yankee soldier who threatened her mother, and he was not her only victim.

Emma Edmonton, on the other hand, did not use feminine wiles, but rather disguised herself as a male Union soldier named Frank Thompson. Like Belle, she was a sharpshooter and participated in some of the bloodiest battles, witnessing brutal carnage. Emma was devoted to Gen. George McClellan, a brilliant strategist, skilled engineer, and "military wunderkind" who believed he had been chosen by God to save the Union.

125

Throughout her military service, Emma would share her secret with only one person, Jerome Robbins, the chief of the military hospital whose aide she would become, assisting with amputations, comforting the wounded and dying. Emma was later enlisted as a spy and she relished the dangerous missions, such as sneaking into Yorktown disguised as a Negro slave having mastered a convincing slave dialect. Her job was to determine the number of Confederate troops stationed there. On another occasion her disguise as an Irish peasant allowed her to eavesdrop on enemy soldiers lingering in town while pretending to shop in the stores where they gathered. The information these women obtained and the services they rendered were invaluable to the success of the armies.

Equally smart and plucky was Elizabeth Van Lew, a wealthy spinster who abhorred slavery. Receiving permission from a Confederate general to visit Union prisoners, she devised a way of passing information on notes hidden in cakes and breads she brought them. The wooden butt of a pistol was hidden between soft gingerbread cookies, the barrel pushed into a loaf of bread. She also made gifts of books whose pages contained tediously encoded messages written with pinpricks. She even arranged to have her Princeton educated slave Mary Jane become a servant in the Confederate White House of Jefferson Davis in order to procure information about the Southern army. Moreover, she ran the Richmond Underground like a well-oiled, well-organized government body. Once under suspicion, she was kept prisoner in her own home, but continued to hide wounded Union soldiers in a secret room and assisted in their escape at night.

The fourth zealous and committed female spy was Rose O'Neal Greenhow, possibly the most out-spoken and brazenly defiant. Head of Washington's Confederate spy ring, she had many admirers since she was slim, attractive, and alluring. Her clever wit and savvy were as much a draw as her figure. One Union colonel called her "one of the most persuasive women ever known in the capital city." Jefferson Davis concurred that "no woman knew more men of power and influence, both North and South, as she."

Rose was so shrewd that she frustrated and thwarted even the well-known Detective Pinkerton who was hired to trail her and keep eye on all her comings and goings. Eventually, she was caught and accused of treason for warning and aiding the enemy with information about the Battle of Bull Run. Demands were made for her release, but Gen. McClellan objected saying "she knew his plans better than Pres. Lincoln." Banned from returning to her beloved South, Rose went to Europe seeking support for the Southern cause from Napoleon himself. Fearful of capture and execution, she drowned when abandoning the ship carrying her back to the US while it was being pursued by a Union vessel.

Emma (alias Frank Thompson eventually penned her memoirs entitled *Unsexed; or, The Female Soldier* describing in detail her valor during the war's deadliest battles. It was a huge success, "the greatest publishing phenomenon of the 19th century." She donated all of the proceeds to the sick and wounded soldiers of The Army of the Potomac.

Belle Boyd took to the stage after the war, riding horseback and dramatizing scenes reminiscent of her exploits.

Elizabeth was rewarded for her service to her country by being appointed postmaster of Richmond by Pres. Ulysses Grant -- one of the highest federal offices a woman could hold in the 19th century, but she was shunned by Southerners who considered her a traitor.

This is history that reads like adventure -- a dramatic narration of the derring-do of incredibly clever and indomitable women who risked their families, their reputations, their very lives for the cause in which they believed. They were fearless and intrepid, committed and worthy adversaries who used all within their power to dupe and foil the enemy. With a dramatic flair, this book tells the stories of these unsung and admirable heroines.

UNDER MAGNOLIA:
A SOUTHERN MEMOIR

by
Frances Mayes

The well-known author of *Under the Tuscan Sun* and *Every Day in Tuscany*, Frances Mayes has, in *Under Magnolia,* turned her thoughts to her birthplace of Fitzgerald, Georgia where she was raised by a hard- drinking and unpredictable father, Grabert, together with a bitter and disillusioned mother Frankeye. Probably the greatest strength of this book is Mayes' ability to create an acutely palpable feeling of "place" through her direct appeal to the senses. For example, reminiscences of her home town are stirred by the "narcotizing fragrance of the land -- jasmine, ginger lilies, wisteria, gardenia blending with honeysuckle, the scent entangled with the euphonious chorus of tree frogs and the mouthy baritone of swamp frogs croaking contrapuntal ... Only here can I step outside and, by merely inhaling say, 'Lawd o' mercy.'" Through her acutely vivid descriptions, the reader can visualize the blossoming magnolia, the towering oaks, pecan, and sycamore trees, the crepe-myrtle, "the hedges of arching bridal wreath all creating a sun-spangled leaf canopy shading the white-wrap-around porch."

A true child of the South, she compares those elements of Georgia and North Carolina, where she also spent time, with those that first attracted her to Tuscany (Italy), among them, the warmth of the Italian people who resembled the "y'all come hospitality" of her native Southerners. In addition, was their mutual emphasis on ancestors and the past, interconnection of family and friends, incessant talking, storytelling, and a sense of fatalism.

Her story, however, is not all beauty and roses. Hers was a difficult childhood. Both parents were restless, bored, and unhappy. There were constant shouting matches, jealous rages, and recriminations; both drank to excess; her father often threatened with a loaded gun, and Frances became the scapegoat of their anger and frustration. The only calm, steady, and levelheaded presence in her life was her beloved black nanny Willie Bell. While Frances' mother ignored her, Willie Bell consoled and encouraged her. "Don't mind them none," she would say. "They's crazy." It was Willie Bell, who tapping the child's shoulder blades, would say, "You got wings back here; you gon' fly, little girl." Sometimes in order to escape the chaos at home, Frances would follow the nanny to the tarpapered shack, where Willie Bell lived on the edge of town.

There is a lot to glean from this book. First of all, it is a character study of an extremely dysfunctional family and their complex relationships with each other. Moreover, it provides a very personal and firsthand depiction of the South -- its rampant racism; its relentless, oppressive and suffocating heat that causes both dogs and humans to go mad; its emphasis on tradition, family ancestry, courtesy, and manners; remnants and reminders of the Civil War; men in white linen suits sipping mint juleps and escorting their daughters to coming-out balls; signs with "Repent" nailed to trees; black rag dolls that become white when turned upside down.

Ms. Mayes' goal throughout her entire childhood and young adulthood was to escape what her mother lamented was "the end of the earth," and Frances did achieve that. Read this totally absorbing book to learn how she accomplished this and went on to become a successful author.

WILD:
FROM LOST TO FOUND ON THE PACIFIC CREST TRAIL

by
Cheryl Strayed

The girl with the hole in her heart

The author of this book, Cheryl Strayed, was wild with rage, anger and pain following the loss of her mother who succumbed to cancer at age forty five. Growing up in a poverty-stricken, fractured family that constantly moved from one shabby place to another, the author had been torn by conflicting emotions for most of her young life. Totally adrift, disgusted and disillusioned with the path her life had taken -- one-night stands with men she barely knew, alcohol and drug use -- she was at the nadir of her existence when she happened upon a guide book about hiking the Pacific Crest Trail. Hardly prepared either physically or emotionally for such an arduous expedition, she felt she had nothing more to lose that she cared about.

So begins her punishing, grueling, tortured hike over extremely rough terrain -- dry creek beds and jagged gullies in scorching temperatures reaching over one hundred degrees, but tempered by majestic mountains, towering trees, and gurgling brooks. It is a treacherous and dangerous undertaking, where at times she encounters black bears and rattlesnakes, and even loses her hiking boots over the mountain side. Her extremely heavy backpack, which becomes an appendage she names "The Monster," cuts into her hips, shoulders, and tail-bone rubbing them raw; her feet develop bleeding blisters, causing her intense pain. Her ascent is a relentless assault on her lungs and heart, her muscles ache, and at times she is shivering -- chilled inside of her sweat-soaked clothes. At one point she has no source of water and is seriously dehydrated. Her hope is that this agonizing experience might have a cathartic effect on her battered spirit, purging her of her past mistakes and misdeeds. Read

131

this heart-rending account of how this ordeal in the wild is curative, setting her on the right track both literally and figuratively, so that at its end she is able to say that the hole in her heart feels "infinitesimally smaller."

CONFESSIONS OF A SURGEON:
THE GOOD, THE BAD, AND THE COMPLICATED LIFE BEHIND THE OR DOORS

by

Paul Ruggieri, MD

More than 30 million people in the United States undergo surgery each year. This book is about the making of the surgeons who operate on this population. It is a very candid account of the insecurities, lack of preparedness, trepidation, and errors of these doctors in training as they hone their skills. Being able to think quickly on one's feet, make quick evaluations despite exhausting hours on duty, stress and fatigue are all part of the rigorous routine. The stakes, of course, are high, the environment chaotic, and errors are made by even the most experienced physicians. In the I980s the publication of the landmark paper "To Err is Human" concluded that 44,000 - 98,000 patients died each year due to medical errors in hospitals. The result of that report was the initiation of reforms that would reduce that number. The duration of time on duty was reduced, for one, since an unrealistic workload and sleep deprivation were believed accountable for part of these sobering statistics. The author, a surgeon himself, admits to his own share of complications but asserts that a skilled surgeon knows how to get himself out of situations he may have caused by an inadvertent slip of the very sharp instrument he may be using. Excessive bleeding, for example, can create a continuous liquid pool in which the doctor cannot clearly see the organ on which he is operating. Ruggieri says that becoming a competent surgeon involves three periods: the first ten years when a surgeon learns how to operate; the second ten years when a surgeon learns when to operate (he becomes more selective); and the third ten years when he learns when not to operate, as when patients are too ill to withstand the trauma to their bodies.

He goes on to describe other traits a surgeon must acquire: the ability to contain emotions as they will only serve to distract him at critical times; the ability to deal with unpredictable situations, which are constant; the ability to be candid about failures as well as successes. Dr. Ruggieri predicts that there will be an extreme shortage of doctors in the next ten to fifteen years. High medical school tuitions leave the young doctors in debt for years to come; low Medicare and Medicaid payments do not compensate the doctors adequately for their skills, hours on call, and ability to earn a respectable living; the numerous guidelines and regulations of the Joint Committee on Accreditation of Healthcare Organization (JCAHO has lessened their autonomy (too many bureaucrats are telling them what they can and cannot do, as with ordering diagnostic tests, as well as how much time they are allowed to spend with a patient; the prohibitive cost of escalating malpractice insurance, as every patient becomes a potential law suit. For these reasons the book ends on a note of bitterness and frustration. He began his career with a gung-ho attitude which has been tempered by real-life experience. I applaud him for telling us how it is.

MY BELOVED WORLD

by
Sonia Sotomayor

From Barrio to US Supreme Court

This is an inspiring story of not only survival, but also amazing achievement. Born in a poor neighborhood where prostitution, gangs, and drug use were rampant, Sonia Sotomayor also suffered from an extremely unhappy home environment full of turmoil and recrimination. Hers was the humblest of beginnings further disadvantaged by her father's alcoholism. While such adversity might have cowered a less resilient and independent child, in Sonia it heightened her awareness of behavior and its consequences, the problems inherent in poverty and lack of opportunity, bias and bigotry, and urban social problems. Despite her total lack of role models to emulate, she knew at a very young age that education was paramount to success and applied herself with relentless hours to that end. One rather interesting memory from her childhood was her love of the Perry Mason TV series where she was first introduced to the world of courts and lawyers. Even at that young age, it was the role of the judge -- calm, impartial, in control -- that most appealed to her, perhaps a very early harbinger of her future goal. Eventually her devotion to study led to scholarships to a number of Ivy League institutions. A greater problem than gaining acceptance to these prestigious universities was getting there for the interviews. Stanford was out of the question since she could never afford the plane travel. So with coins and a few dollars scraped together, she managed by bus and train to visit those within reasonable distance to NY, her home. The interviews brought further dismay as she discovered, as in the case of Radcliffe (Harvard's sister school) that she was so intimidated by the opulent surroundings and what seemed such an alien setting, she became convinced that she could never fit in. Eventually she chose Princeton, but even there she felt that she did not belong -- "a stranger in a strange land." Because she had gained entry through affirmative action, she was sometimes made to feel like an interloper, unworthy of the opportunity bestowed upon her. As a result, she worked harder and harder to compensate for what she knew to be the gaps in her background. For example, although her intellect was keen, her written work was riddled with grammatical errors as well as Spanish constructions and usage, not surprising for one raised in a Spanish speaking family. More troubling for her than these deficiencies, for which she compensated by studying grammar texts and learning ten new vocabulary words each day, were the cultural gaps. She had never seen the richness of Oriental carpets, the smart and expensive attire of most of her classmates, the ease with which they mixed socially, their European travel and trust funds. Even as an accomplished adult many years later, she retained this sense of inferiority when surrounded by wealth and prestige. Fortunately, Ms. Sotomayor had the strength of character, the wisdom gained from a lifetime of adversity, the innate intelligence, determination and work ethic to not only overcome such limitations of background, but also to succeed to the high level of appointment to the United States Supreme Court. She is a living example of "The American Dream" at its best!

ELSEWHERE:
A MEMOIR

by
Richard Russo

His Mother Followed Him to College

Some mothers have become famous for their obsessive connection to their sons; Sara Delano Roosevelt, for example, in her relationship to her adored Franklin. But the bond that existed between Richard Russo, *New York Times* Best-selling author, and his mother extended a lifetime and beyond the physical severing of the umbilical cord at birth. In reality, the emotional and psychological attachment to her son was this single mother's lifeline. Unable to tolerate more than a few hours or few miles separation from him, she found her comfort level -- her very sanity -- dependent on her proximity to him. So begins the story of the intricate and ongoing waltz between them, even after his marriage, with his mother following in her son's footsteps wherever his career took him.

Unaware of his mother's crippling personality disorder, he supports her often irrational jolts through life, thus unwittingly becoming her enabler. *Elsewhere* is a fascinating story of a son's devotion to his dysfunctional parent and her singularly abnormal dependence on him.

IDENTICAL STRANGERS

by

Elyse Schien & Paula Bernstein

A memoir, *Identical Strangers,* is a fascinating story of identical twin girls separated after birth and adopted by two different families, both of whom were unaware that each child had a sibling. It took thirty years for the sisters to find each other and together investigate their shared parentage and the circumstances of their birth. Their first meeting is fraught with ambivalence -- excitement and anticipation tinged with fear and anxiety. As they face each other, they feel "like strangers inhabiting the same body." Gradually they become acquainted and are incredulous to observe shared characteristics: animated hand movements when speaking, dramatic facial expressions; even the same speech cadence and inflection. In addition, both have chosen careers in film and suffer from depression, as well as migraine headaches. Such similarities are known to be common among identical twins since they share the exact same DNA; essentially they are clones of each other. Their joint search for answers regarding their biological parents brings them to Louise Wise Services, the once-prestigious Jewish adoption agency in New York City. Although those at Louise Wise are evasive and guarded, the sisters eventually learn through other sources that they were initially part of a study researching the inheritance of mental illness, since their mother had been schizophrenic. Outraged that they were used as pawns for study and that their adoptive parents never agreed to this, they begin to assiduously search for other sets of twins separated and placed for adoption by this same agency. This book is replete with well-known studies conducted by the prominent experts in the '60s – '80s who found remarkably similar traits between twins and triplets raised in different locations by different families. The "Jim Twins" in Ohio, for example, when reunited after thirty plus years, learned that they both drove the same type of Chevrolet; chain-smoked Salem cigarettes; gnawed at their fingernails; had the same IQ's and identical weight; liked stock car racing, woodworking, and football; suffered from high blood pressure; married women named Linda and after divorcing, married women named Betty; both had sons they named James Allan; and served as sheriff's deputies in nearby Ohio counties. They only found each other when a friend of one brother mentioned that there was someone in a nearby county who looked just like him. Another set known as "the firemen twins" were Mark Newman and Jerry Levy, both bal d, six foot four inch brothers reunited at age thirty one to find they both enjoyed deep-sea fishing and drinking beer which they held by placing their pinky finger beneath the bottle. Both had been interested in a career in forestry before taking jobs installing electrical equipment. Both chose to become volunteer firemen who became captains of their separate squads the same year. Moreover, on an IQ test they scored only two points apart. And the list goes on and on. Another pair, Tony Milasi and Roger Brooks -- the first raised in a traditional Catholic home in NY and the second in a Jewish family in Miami -- used the same brand of Swedish toothpaste, smoked Lucky Strikes, liked the same music, parted their hair on the left, loved sports, entered separate branches of the military four days apart for four year enlistments, were confirmed bachelors and were naturally optimistic, despite Roger's difficult childhood. This is one amazing story, factual as it cites well-documented research, as well as emotional as the two sister-authors struggle to gain knowledge about their past and attempt to bond after so many years apart. The reader joins them in expectation as they attempt to piece together the puzzle of their mutual heritage.

PRIMATES OF PARK AVENUE

by

Wednesday Martin

When Mid-Westerner Wednesday Martin moves with her husband and toddler to Manhattan's Upper East Side, she experiences culture shock. Socially and culturally, it is an entirely opposite environment from the West Village, her former location. She feels like a misfit -- ignored and disdained by the clique of designer-clad, ultra-thin, perfectly sculptured "tribe" of mommies at her child's pre-school. Mean, arrogant, and aggressive, they seem to vie for dominance, even on the sidewalk; one woman actually charges right by her, knocking her aside with a $15,000 Hermes Birken handbag. Wanting to assimilate and win acceptance, Martin becomes a keen observer of their style: in winter, sporty fur jackets by Givenchy and Saint Laurent, complemented by leather or suede boots by Blahnik, Jimmy Choo, or Louboutin; in summer, ballet flats by Lanvin, Chanel, or Chloe. In her frenzy to be recognized, this low-maintenance woman resorts to asking her husband for a Birken as a special gift, only to find that there is a three year waiting list. Martin is very aware that she is succumbing to the "apex of frivolity" but still covets this costly accessory that she views as a sword and shield in this hostile female world. In an attempt to understand what is happening to her and also how these women became so superficial, she resorts to her earlier courses in anthropology while in college and graduate school. Recalling studies by prominent researchers who focused on various animal species, Martin begins to see a similarity between the rites and behavior of her East Side contemporaries with their "animal sisters," particularly baboons, and realizes that these women resemble primates in their quest for power and territory. One study on which she focuses was Jane Goodall's work with the chimps of Goomba where Goodall keenly observed a chimp she named "Mike" who managed to get his paws on two empty, discarded, metal kerosene containers with handles. With this, his own type of

141

"Birken," he charged at the other troops, banging and swinging them like scepters. In utter awe, the other chimps scattered, allowing Mike to maintain his dominance for five years. Martin comes to believe that both the chimps of West Africa and these New York mommies have their tribal ways, as do those primates in the Amazon jungle or Mayan villages in Mexico.

You might be surprised to learn that when the author suffers a personal tragedy, some of these initially callous, unfriendly, and dismissive women will be the very ones to empathize and support her emotionally. This rallying to the aid of the weaker member also leads her to recall other studies of primatologists who recorded this same compassion demonstrated in animals who cared for each other when the need arose.

In this book the author employs a very clever technique in equating human and animal behavior, including what factors cause anxiety, how participants compete for dominance, and how grooming and preening are used in similar ways to attract mates.

This should not be derided as a gossipy, vengeful satire; rather it is a highly intelligent assessment of what she encountered and even willingly participated in, while she resided among them. Scholarly in its reference to so many authentic scientific studies, *Primates of Park Avenue* is not only amusing, but also insightful and enlightening.

LOTS OF CANDLES, PLENTY OF CAKE

by

Anna Quindlen

I unabashedly love Anna Quindlen. I do not share her political bent; but since "I am a woman of a certain age," she resonates with me. I have followed her career from the beginning when she was a young writer for *The New York Times*, and I have all of her articles compiled in two collections, *Living Out Loud* and *Thinking Out Loud*. In addition, I have read all of her novels, the most powerful, *One True Thing*, which became the heart-rending film by the same title with Meryl Streep playing a terminally-ill wife and mother and Renee Zellweger, her daughter, who has been summoned home to care for her. Quindlen has insisted that this novel is not auto-biographical; but knowing her personal history, I assume that certain portions must be. I sobbed throughout both the book and the movie, two of the most emotionally taxing, vicarious experiences of my life.

Lots of Candles, Plenty of Cake is very different in subject matter but has been criticized by one reviewer as being too similar in style to her former newspaper columns in which Quindlen has "found a formula which works for her and which she uses repeatedly." Each chapter in this book derives from events in her own life -- from childhood to successful career woman to manic motherhood to mature woman approaching sixty. Some chapters, such as "Generations," elicit strong feelings as she recalls her mother's drafting table abandoned in the basement, as she gave birth to child after child, and succumbed to cancer at an early age, never realizing the potential she demonstrated as a young professional. Anna never knew her mother harbored desires or dreams beyond motherhood. In that same section, Quindlen describes herself as "a know-it-all rising star" early in her journalistic career, feeling indomitable on her rise up the ladder, when an older female colleague told her,

"You should never forget that you will only have as much power as (men are willing to give you."

There are chapters on "Solitude" and "Mirror, Mirror" which deal with aging and subsequent body changes. She quotes the actor Kevin Bacon who says, "The good news is that the eyes and face go about the same time, so you can't see how you look." And I also identified with her description of her knee "making a sound like Rice Krispies when she squats," a very appropriate analogy. She candidly discusses her earlier problem with alcohol and its negative effect on her behavior and personality. For her, giving it up was a "life saver."

There's a lot here to contemplate if, like Anna Quindlen and myself, you are approaching a certain age. As to this fact, she says, "I am no longer young and certainly not elderly. I am past the mid-point of my life. I am at a good point in my life." I say, "Me too!"

JERRY LEE LEWIS:
HIS OWN STORY

by

Rick Bragg

WOW! What a story! What a life! Crazy. Wild. Frenzied. Dangerous. On-the-edge. Raucous. These adjectives do not adequately capture the essence of the legendary Rock 'n' Roll musician Jerry Lee Lewis. Even the term "musician" does not do his talent justice. For whether one liked or deplored his outrageous antics both on and off the stage -- he once poured and ignited a can of Coke filled with kerosene onto the piano while playing his famous hit "Great Balls of Fire" -- anyone who ever saw him perform could not deny his artistic genius, improvisation, and uniqueness. Born dirt poor to uneducated tenant farmers in rural Louisiana, Lewis revealed that he was a musical prodigy at age five when, in his aunt's living room, he climbed up on a piano bench and began playing Gospel hymns heard in church and songs his mother sang to him. His description of this moment, in his own words, is remarkable -- almost miraculous -- as he experienced a "strange something that he felt in his entire body. The first key sounded in his head, ringing and ringing, and told his fingers what to do. It kept happening, like a cascade." He has never remembered wanting to touch something so badly in his whole life, and yet he didn't even know what this big, black instrument was. The hold it took upon his life and senses was overwhelming. He no longer wanted to go to school, no longer wanted to do anything but play and play all day and into the late night. His Daddy, who owned nothing but a beat-up truck, had mortgaged it to get him a piano, which was a monumental feat in itself, since "only rich men had pianos." I suppose one could say the rest is history -- but what a history! And Rick Bragg is the perfect storyteller for Jerry Lee. His style is so easy and laid-back -- conversational -- as if the reader is sitting in the living room listening as Lewis describes his topsy-turvy life, reeling from highs to lows, on top of the musical charts one day, banned from the radio the next. All his life he admits

to being a rascal, "I just done what I wanted," totally ignoring rules and regulations, laws and paperwork. If he wanted a car, he just drove it off the lot,
"but always returned it." So it is not surprising that when he wanted to replace one
wife with another, he never bothered to apply for a divorce; that when he
received a draft notice, as did his fellow star Elvis Presley, he simply tore it up
and discarded it; and that when he wanted to marry his 13 year-old cousin,
he simply did so, despite the warnings and advice of his agents and
"handlers," telling them that "nobody handles Jerry Lee Lewis." It was this
marriage, his third out of a total of seven, that derailed his career just
when he had reached the acme of the music world. A long-planned tour to
England in the 1950s was over before it started, once the scandal labeled him
a "per-vert" and "baby-snatcher." Even in the US stations refused to play his
songs which in some cases were banned from the airways. But there is no
denying he was a "PHENOMENON" -- a brilliant musician -- explosive,
dynamic, and fierce -- as talented as the best -- Johnny Cash, Hank Williams,
Jimmie Rodgers, even Elvis himself. Bragg narrates so many interesting
anecdotes involving Lewis' interaction with these "greats," many of whom
started out with "gos-pel," "blues," and "country" which they adapted it their
own style. This is one mighty good read, particularly for anyone interested in the
history of "Rock 'n' Roll," but also for those looking for a "howlin" good read,
which is exactly what this "species unto himself" did his entire career –
howlin' and stompin' and thumpin' his way to legendary musical heights.

BILL O'REILLY'S LEGENDS AND LIES:
THE REAL WEST

by
David Fisher

The American West of the 1800s was a sweeping territory -- a lawless and dangerous place which required hardiness, stamina, resilience, courage, shrewdness, and cunning to survive. These were traits shared by many of the characters depicted in *Bill O'Reilly's Legends & Lies.* In addition, these "heroes" honed their skills to become expert hunters, trackers, explorers, and marksmen. If you grew up in the 1950s when Western movies and TV shows were popular, you will recognize many of the names that appear in this book, namely Wild Bill Hickock, Billy the Kid, Jesse James, Kit Carson, Gen. Armstrong Custer, and "The Lone Ranger," to mention only a few. What you might not know is that the real "The Lone Ranger" was a black American named Bass Reeves who was born into slavery in 1858 but became a freeman in Texas with the issuance of *The Emancipation Proclamation*. He eventually settled in Oklahoma, learned the languages of five Indian tribes, was a skilled tracker and horseman, and a dead-shot, both right and left-handed. It was such a wild territory that an outlaw Dick Glass once killed a man in a disagreement over an ear of corn! Reeves became a US Marshall who was known for his integrity and sense of fair play; and it was said that after capturing his fugitives, he would tie them to a log and preach the Gospel to them. Although Reeves didn't wear a mask, he used many disguises. He was often accompanied by an Indian officer from the reservation, who might have been his faithful sidekick "Tonto." In addition, he was known to give a silver dollar to witnesses who helped him; hence, the basis for the legendary silver bullet "The Lone Ranger" was said to leave behind.

Another intriguing character was Charles Earl Bowles, otherwise known as "Black Bart, The Gentleman Bandit." He limited himself to robberies of Wells Fargo stagecoaches – twenty eight in all. He had originally been a gold miner, but when two men from that company bought the land above his stake and cut off this water supply needed to pan gold, he swore retribution by holding up twenty-nine Wells Fargo transports with impunity. However, when one panicked passenger threw her purse out the window of the coach he was robbing, he returned it saying, "Madame, I do not wish to take your money ... only that of Wells Fargo." In all other respects he was a refined man, perfectly groomed, living and dining in grand hotels, and wearing a bowler hat and linen suit with a diamond in his lapel, even during his hold-ups. Wells Fargo reassured their passengers that "Black Bart" never demonstrated viciousness and was averse to taking human life." Rather unusual for men of his ilk was his fear of horses, which he avoided entirely. Unable to ride, he planned his strategy carefully so that he was able to traverse on foot before and after the hold-ups. Moreover, he left poems at the sites of his crimes:

"I've labored long and hard for bread, For honor and for riches
But on my corns too long you've tread You fine-hair'd sons-of-b.........s"

Another:
"I rob the rich to feed the poor
Which hardly is a sin,
A widow ne'er knocked at my door But what I let her in,
So blame me not for what I've done I don't deserve your curses And if for any cause, I'm hung
Let it be for my verses.

There are many other interesting tidbits:
The outlaw Jesse James was the son of a Baptist preacher. After Jesse's death, his mother, ever a practical woman, sold pebbles from his grave as souvenirs, always replenishing them at the end of each day to satisfy the steady stream of tourists. Her other son, Frank James, loved Shakespeare and had dreams of going to college. Both boys were emotionally scarred and damaged by the atrocities of The Civil War. They had been mentored by the inhumane Southern guerrilla fighter "Bloody Bill Anderson" who had witnessed his father

hanged by the Union militiamen and his three sisters savagely treated when taken as hostages. His anger and revenge led him to torture captives, scalp them and cut off their ears. After participation in such atrocities, there was no hope that any of these boys could once again assimilate and return to civilized life.

O'Reilly's book is replete with interesting facts: Kit Carson, the eleventh of fifteen children in his family, was only five foot four inches," yet he was considered the most intimidating Indian fighter in the West, who earlier in his career had crawled through enemy Mexican lines to run thirty miles barefoot to save his besieged comrade soldiers. In the end, Carson, usually dressed in homespun buckskins, was dismayed by what he came to see as the unfair treatment of the Indians. For example, in 1865 Kit told a Congressional committee, "I came to this country in 1826 and I am pretty well- acquainted with Indian tribes, both in peace and at war, and I think, as a general thing, the difficulties arise from aggressions on the part of the whites." Confirming Carson's observation was Chief Black Hawk's assertion upon his tribe's surrender in 1832: "We told them to leave us alone, and keep away from us; but they followed on, and beset our paths, and they coiled themselves among us, like a snake. They poisoned us with their touch."

Another renowned Indian fighter was Gen. Armstrong Custer who was known for his flamboyant, extravagant uniforms: a black velvet jacket with gold lace and brass buttons topped by a brilliant crimson necktie tied in a graceful knot at his throat; a wide-brimmed hat over his long, flowing blond hair treated with cinnamon oil. Sometimes he wore a white, fringed buckskin jacket, now enshrined in The Smithsonian so that his "troops could easily identify him during a battle." Despite his valor in war, riding always at the front of his men, becoming legendary for having thirteen horses shot from under him, with nary a scratch on his body, awesome in the thick of battle striking to left and right, he had not shown the characteristics of a good leader early on. At West Point "Cinnamon," as he was nicknamed, compiled 726 demerits for his mischievous antics and academically finished at the very bottom of his class. "But no one questioned his bravery," although some other officers considered him "arrogant and vain."

Along with these historical facts, too numerous to mention, are truly remarkable photographs, authentic "Wanted" posters, business card portraits, real estate ads for "Indian Land for Sale," historic lithographs of famous battle scenes, personal letters, documents and maps -- all of which greatly enhance the information presented in the book. If you are a fan of "Westerns," adventure, and legendary heroes larger-than-life, this book will appeal to you; but be forewarned, there are some lurid descriptions of bloody attacks and massacres complete with gruesome torture, including scalping. Such was the real Wild West.

Other interesting facts gleaned from *Bill O'Reilly's Legends & Lies*":

Annie Oakley made her first shot at eight years-old.

"Buffalo Bill" Cody became a Pony Express rider at age thirteen and claimed to have made the longest journey ever -- 322 miles round trip.

The only authentic photograph of "Billy the Kid," a 2"x3" ferrotype was sold at auction in 2011 for $2.3 million, making it at that time the fourth most valuable photograph in the world.

In Leadville, Colorado where "Doc" Holliday settled in 1883, the sign in the saloon read: "Please do not shoot the pianist. He is doing his best."

John "Doc" Holliday was a wealthy and well-educated man, a very skilled dentist before becoming a gun-toting gambler.

In 1880, Tombstone, Arizona had one hundred and ten saloons, fourteen gambling halls, many brothels, and one bowling alley.

The gun fight at the OK Corral involving "Doc" and the Earp brothers, lasted only thirty seconds but has been the subject of books and films for years. "Doc" has been played by actors Walter Huston, Stacy Keach, Victor Mature, Kirk Douglas, Jason Robards, Val Kilmer, and Dennis Quaid.

Jesse and Frank James changed their last name to Howard and eventually hid out in Mexico. Of those years Frank said, "The quiet and upright life were the happiest I have spent. My old life grew more detestable the further I got away from it." Later both returned to the US and took up their violent lives again, but until the day that Jesse died, his two children did not know their father's real name or identity.

Attacks on wagon trains by Indians were rare. Settlers were more likely to hire them as guides or trade with them.

After negotiating treaties with Indians, the American government broke those pacts when land became valuable.

Some Indian tribes, such as the Iroquois in the North-east part of our country, were highly sophisticated. Hundreds of years before the American Constitution, their Great Law of Peace included freedom of speech and religion, a separation of government powers, and the right of women to participate in government.

CUSTER'S TRIALS
A LIFE ON THE FRONTIER OF NEW AMERICA

by

T. J. Stiles

Custer's Trials is the newest biography on one of the most famous and colorful individuals of the 19th century, Gen. Armstrong Custer, Civil War leader and Indian fighter. A fascinating man of contradictions, he has been considered more of a phenomenon than a person. But in this scholarly, well-researched work, the author T. J. Stiles, a winner of both the Pulitzer and National Book Awards, reveals the authentic human beneath the image. Stiles attempts to integrate Custer's many conflicting parts: a battlefield emancipator on the Northern side in the Civil War while an avowed white supremacist; a loyal friend, loving brother, son, and ardent husband as well as a sarcastic gambler who craved the attention of other women; a widely-admired military professional who was court martialed twice. Despite graduating last in his class at West Point, he was adept in siege techniques, a supreme leader demonstrating good judgment, a brilliant tactician, gallant and ultra-courageous in battle. Although he is most associated with the Battle of Little Bighorn, he caught the public's attention long before that. Even the outlandish uniform he personally crafted screamed for attention and announced his personal bravery: a broad-brimmed hat tilted to one side over his mass of long wavy blond curls, a double-breasted black velveteen jacket with gold piping, eight buttons on each side, embellished with five parallel lines of gold embroidery looped about sleeves from forearm to elbow; and a red scarf around his neck. He chose to stand out even in battle amidst clashing sabers, firing pistols, revolver blasts, stumbling horses, and colliding infantrymen. Some may have found him curious, but he cared not whether others found him laughable or inspiring as he galloped onto the field, swinging his sword, blond hair flying. Both his soldiers and the enemy could spot him easily and he was always at the front leading. Despite his vulnerable position, he was extremely lucky; once a bullet hit

153

his shoulder and bounced off, only bruising him. Another hit his arm but was too spent to do him damage. Although bullets kicked up dust all around him, they always struck someone else to whose aid he would charge and drag back to safety. On one of these rescue missions, he was hit, but the round merely grazed his head, briefly stunning him. Horses were shot from beneath him but he always managed to survive. He was a celebrity, but his penchant for planting political stories against those with whom he disagreed alienated powerful people, including Pres. Ulysses Grant.

Many pages are devoted to his passionate relationship with his wife Libbie who followed him whenever possible on his missions. She basked in the reflected glory of so famous and gallant a man and was proud of his accomplishments. On one occasion he was removed from his post for a year because he deserted his fort in order to visit her. He was found guilty of being absent without leave. This was true to character because he could be impulsive and independent, breaking rules when it suited him. In an ardent missive to her (published in a book of *The 50 Greatest Love Letters of All Time* reviewed here, he vowed that at the moment of his death, her name would bless his lips.

Replete with information about numerous Civil War battles and Western campaigns against the Indians -- some with shockingly savage details -- this book contains adventure and battlefield strategy, as well as romance and psychology.

MRS. KENNEDY AND ME

by
Clint Hill

He Didn't Want the Job

When Clint Hill, FBI agent, was assigned as Mrs. Jacqueline Kennedy's personal body guard upon her husband's election to the Presidency, he was not happy. In fact, he was extremely disappointed, anticipating a continuous whirlwind of teas, receptions, shopping excursions, and other typically feminine activities. After all, he had served on the Secret Service Detail guarding Presidents in what he considered a significant capacity and felt slighted to not continue in that role. Read this very personal account of the development of the relationship between Agent Hill and Mrs. Kennedy as he became her devoted guardian, caretaker, and friend -- a comforting omnipresence to both her and her children throughout her time as First Lady. The one constant in her life during this period, he shared her most significant experiences -- births, miscarriages, family celebrations, vacations -- and, yes, deaths and tragedies as well. He was the one to whom Jackie was reaching in that famous photo of the assassination in Dallas on November 22, 1963 as she climbed upon the trunk of the presidential limo in her blood-stained pink suit. Plagued by guilt after that day, Clint Hill was convinced that had he reacted a bit faster, history might have been different. It was a regret that negatively impacted much of his life and took a great deal of time to overcome.

THE FIRST FAMILY DETAIL

by

Ron Kessler

Prize-winning investigative reporter Ron Kessler seems obsessed with "telling all" details regarding recent presidents, vice presidents, their wives, and their children. *The First Family Detail* is not his first book on this subject, but a very revealing one. Based on numerous interviews with retired FBI and Secret Service, whom he openly identifies and quotes, he has compiled an interesting collection of incidents the agents recall in their work with these families. Some speak volumes about their subjects, some of whom were very much loved and respected by their protectors, others detested. Among those "first families" most loved were the Bushes. Both father and son, George and George W., as well as their wives Barbara and Laura, eschewed leaving the White House at Christmas time so that the agents could spend the holiday with their own families, a kindness for which these men were deeply grateful. (Most other Presidents left immediately before the holiday for their own homes or ranches, with agents in tow to cover them). Moreover, both Barbara and her daughter-in-law Laura were extremely considerate of the sacrifices the agents made on their behalf. When on duty for hours in freezing temperatures outside their homes, Laura would bring them warm coffee and food. Barbara, on one occasion, was so concerned that her agent was not warmly dressed for a winter outing in Maine, that she returned to the house to get him a hat and coat. George, Sr., in a show of support, even had his head shaved when an agent's young son was being treated for leukemia with the resulting hair loss. Others, however, showed little respect and even disdain and annoyance at what they felt was an invasion of their privacy. Hillary Clinton, for one, who was notorious for her foul mouth, was so hostile that the agents were often the undeserving victims of her explosive temper. Her husband Bill was not much better, calling his own aides "stupid" and "morons," even literally physically pushing staff out of his way when agitated. The couple's tempestuous

relationship, with shouting matches and flung objects, was verified by numerous White House maids and butlers. Any agent considered it the worst punish-
ment to be assigned to Hillary. In the most disdainful manner, she asked FBI
agent Guy Copeland, "And where do you buy your suits? JC Penny?" On another occasion she angrily fired an agent whom she demanded carry her luggage. He refused saying his hands and arms needed to be unencumbered in
order to do his job. Fortunately, he was later reinstated. Her husband Bill made
their job more difficult as he had a habitual tendency, immediately upon arrival at an airport, to deplane and make a direct beeline to the most attractive
women in a crowd while the agents were still assessing who might be dangerous. The Clintons' disrespect of the office was reflected in the people they
brought with them from Arkansas whose sloppy habits turned parts of the
White House into a "pizza-parlor" with empty boxes strewn everywhere, ciga-
rette butts ground into the Oriental carpets, and scratches on antique historic
desks from feet resting upon these treasured pieces of furniture. Others who
made their job challenging and frustrating were the daughters of George W.
and Laura Bush who made it a game of eluding the agents, trying to lose them
in bars and nightclubs. Eleanor Mondale, daughter of Walter, would make it a
game of flirting with the younger agents, testing their limits. She and a girl-
friend would make up a list of which agents were "hers" and which were the
"friend's."

In their close contact with their clients, the agents have the opportunity to observe each one's idiosyncrasies. Homeland Security Secretary Tom
Ridge, for example, was one of the cheapest. Rather than buy a daily newspaper for himself at a hotel, he would routinely ask an agent for his. Too frugal
to buy a plane ticket home to Pennsylvania every weekend, he would rely on
an agent to drive him six hours each way. If the owner of a restaurant where
he dined thanked him for his service to the country, he would return the very
next night expecting another "free" meal," as generously given the night before. As for cheapness, Gerald Ford topped their list, tipping a golf caddy on
an exclusive golf course in CA, $1-2 for a full day caddying when the going rate
was $25-50. He also felt $1 sufficient for a bellboy who loaded his bags onto a
cart at the Pierre Hotel, one of the most exclusive in New York City. In a Chi-
cago hotel an agent saw him take all the premium liquor from the room.

Some they felt sorry for -- Richard Nixon holding the pole with both hands while fishing on a friend's yacht. Someone else had baited the line for him and if anything was caught, a staff person would reel it in. Nixon did nothing but watch. One agent called him a "brilliant man, but a sorry figure."

There are so many interesting details and facts in this book of observations:

After the election of Obama, threats against a president rose 400%.

Julie Nixon, daughter of Richard, was the "sweetest" of all their clients.

According to former agent Clark Larsen, Lyndon Johnson who was constantly falling, was the clumsiest, not Gerald Ford.

The biggest spender of tax-payer dollars is Joe Biden, whom agents accuse of costly unnecessary trips back and forth from Washington to his home in Delaware, sometimes twice in the same day only to play golf.

The agents find it ironic that Obama placed Biden in charge of the "Campaign to Cut Government Waste" when Biden uses Air Force II indiscriminately (225 times between March, 2009 and March, 2013), requiring five Navy stewards on board to attend to his every need.

Jimmy Carter was another person who was not what he portrayed to the public. In front of the press, he carried his own garment back (empty) to demonstrate he was a "common man." However, according to Secret Service Agent Baranowski, when not in front of the cameras, Carter handed a full and heavy bag to him. Another agent, John Piasecky, who was on the Carter Detail for more than three years, asserted that Carter was short and rude most of the time, looking right past him when he greeted him with "Good Morning," never responding in any way. He told agents to "not speak to him at all." Carter was the most detested and his young daughter Amy was regarded as "the brattiest." Air Force One steward, Brad Wells saw her throw packages of soda crackers all over the floor of the plane, crush them, and expect the stewards to clean them up. Her much older brother Chip was also the "most disliked" of all Presidents' children -- out of control -- smoking marijuana, consuming liquor, chasing women, bringing them into the White house for sex without proper clearance.

Yes, this book is gossipy and probably defies the unspoken rule that White House employees are entrusted to keep what they observe and hear confidential. However, some of the behavior they have witnessed is so egregious as to "loosen" their tongues. Since most of it is documented with the names and verbatim comments of these former employees, it is my opinion that most of what Kessler has recorded is accurate. Lest you think I have covered all there is to be known, let me assure you there is so much more intriguing information in this book about those whom we ourselves have elected to the highest office in the land. I believe that "actions speak louder than words" (forgive the cliché!, and that the behavior of these often- revered men reveals their true characters, some extremely disappointing and dismaying, others worthy of our respect. I leave it to you, the reader, to judge for yourself.

THE RESIDENCE:
INSIDE THE PRIVATE WORLD OF THE WHITE HOUSE

by

Kate Andersen Brower

Many Americans are curious about the residents, their activities, and the staff who occupy The White House in Washington, D.C. It is to us what Buckingham Palace is to the Brits. This book *The Residence* by Kate Brower does much to satisfy that curiosity. Relying on extensive research, in addition to numerous interviews with former Presidents, their wives, and families, as well as butlers, maids, chefs, florists, doormen, painters, carpenters and plumbers who have worked there, the author acquaints us with the inner workings of this revered building, a national treasure. For the staff and those they serve, loyalty, devotion, and discretion are the three most valued traits. This is not a "tell-all" book as is Ron Kessler's *The First Family Detail.* Although the workers have been witness to both stately and dignified behavior by members of First Families, they have also seen shenanigans, usually by the younger set. Most dismissed it as typical teens in the difficult process of growing up in a sort of magnified fish tank. If anything the White House workers seem to empathize with the difficult situation of normal kids thrown into the limelight as the result of their father becoming President. It seems that each worker had a favorite President and some of their memories of interactions with that particular man were heart-warming and sincere. Operations Supervisor Tony Savoy, Houseman Linsey Little, and Chef Roland Mesnier were most fond of George H. Walker and Barbara Bush, Mesnier calling Barbara a "woman with a heart of gold" while Savoy said "she treated all staffers like she was their grandmother." (Savoy sometimes worked a solid month without a day off). They all appreciated that the Bushes took special care to insure that on Christmas all had time to spend with their families, a kindness also appreciated by Secret Service Agents quoted in Kessler's book. In fact, many of the incidents mentioned in Kessler's book were confirmed by White House staffers who observed the same. Workers were aware, for example, of Jimmy Carter's sons using marijuana in The Residence and one of the staff was told by the president to keep his mother Miss Lillian "away from alcohol." Also confirmed by eyewitness accounts were "the pitched battles and vicious cursing" of the Clintons, even one incident with Bill bleeding profusely from the head which required several stitches. One worker said, "We were pretty sure she (Hillary clocked him with a book" resting on her bedside table. All saw Nancy Reagan's "complete and genuine devotion" to her husband, although some like Chief Housekeeper Christine Limerick reluctantly admitted to the author that this First Lady "could be very hard to please." Once when Nancy ordered Chef Mesnier to make an extremely complicated, time-consuming dessert for a state dinner, he said he had only two days left to prepare it. Smiling, she reminded him, "Roland, you have two days AND TWO NIGHTS." On another such occasion again driving him crazy about a certain dessert, her husband (The president said, "Honey, leave the chef alone. That's a beautiful dessert." She replied, "Ronnie, eat your soup; this is not your concern." Looking down at his bowl, he finished the soup without another word." Cletus Clark, the painter who told her two days were not sufficient to repaint all the walls as she had instructed, was told, "I'm sure YOU'LL FIND A WAY." Lyndon Johnson was also known to be demanding and bullying. He would run through the different shops in the basement shouting out a letter grade as would a teacher to his students. One day he told Cliber, the Head Electrician, "Today you got an F!" Another time LBJ was furious that his favorite dessert, cheese blintzes made and sent to the White House by Defense Secretary Robert McNamara's wife, were disposed of since they did not go through the proper screening for food safety, but just handed by McNamara to a police officer who handed them to a Secret Service Agent. "YOU LEAVE MY FOOD ALONE!" he shouted at the agent. Use that thing on the top of your head that's supposed to have a brain. Did you think the Secretary of Defense is going to kill me!" Also verified was Johnson's habit of appearing nude in front of maids and giving orders to staffers while sitting on the toilet. For the most part, however, this book is gentler than Kessler's. Most of the butlers, maids, and valets expressed pride in their jobs as well as their sincere desire to serve the First Families and make them as comfortable as they could.

They did not resent the fact that usually their job took precedence over all else, robbing them of holidays with their families, often missing graduations, birthdays; being on call at all hours, unable to leave their post until all were in bed at The Residence - sometimes until 4 a.m. and 5 a.m. -- only to have to return a few hours later. By and large, most accepted this as "part of the job," knowing the demands when they signed on and choosing to stay. They considered theirs a sacred post, committed to service and proud to be serving, despite the personal sacrifices. They became extremely close to certain individuals, cried with them during tragedies, did all in their power to comfort and sustain them, and felt it the highest privilege to be among these esteemed leaders. Read of the others who kept the White House running from the time of the Kennedys to the current Obamas.

LADY BIRD AND LYNDON:
THE HIDDEN STORY OF A MARRIAGE
THAT MADE A PRESIDENT

by

Betty Boyd Caroli

Marriages make interesting subjects, but high-power political marriages involve even more intriguing relationships. That of Lyndon Baines Johnson and Claudia "Bird" Taylor was one of the most complex. In this very readable analysis of what brought them together and what solidified their union, the author Betty Caroli relies on observations of those closest to them -- aides, friends, family, employees, but most importantly Lady Bird's diaries and interviews, some of which were not open to the public until recently (2014). What initially attracted "Bird" to this dynamo was his energy, determination, ambition, and charisma, but what bound her to him for a lifetime was his need for her; she was essential to him. After a very brief but intense courtship in which he pressured her to quickly accept his marriage proposal, her usual caution and level-headedness was overruled by his powerful magnetism. From the outset, he made it clear to her that he was a very needy man seeking a devoted partner to provide him with limitless nurturing support to help him achieve his goals which were considerable. Looking for an exciting and adventurous life far from rural and sleepy Karnack, Texas where she was born, she "hitched her wagon to his star." It was a whirlwind ride as he rose in the ranks of political power from Congressman to President of the United States, always with her as his cheerleader. But Lyndon was often moody, restless, easily angered, testy, and insecure given to periods of deep depression from which only she could rouse him from his gloom. A bully and a curmudgeon, he could be mean, cruel and belittling in his remarks, alienating those closest to him; and it was she who constantly repaired injured feelings maintaining a powerful network of friends and supporters to remain with him. While he was temperamental, rash, and impulsive, she was the more grounded. When feeling misunderstood or unappreciated, he would lash out while she remained unruffled. Her social skills and natural grace smoothed over his rough edges. Often the scapegoat for his disappointments as well as victim of his infidelities, she chose to ignore his crass behavior, even inviting the women into her home, including them in family dinners and outings. When friends were appalled by what they considered abuse -- even her daughters complained that she was overly "complaisant" to Lyndon's needs and too tolerant of his outrageous demands, she pointed out that he was her life and it was the synergy of their partnership. Later in life she acknowledged that she could have been a better parent, that she had always put her husband first since he demanded her presence at all times, leaving her girls on the periphery with caretakers or babysitters. The greatest stress came during the Vietnam War when the President reached the breaking point. His doctors and aides questioned his mental state and what effect it had on his decision-making when under stress. Some used the term manic-depressive, bi-polar, and paranoid because his behavior patterns fit these diagnoses.

This is a revealing and perceptive story of the woman married to a flawed but brilliant politician, one who accomplished significant legislation, including passage of the Civil Rights Act and Head Start for the underprivileged, to name only two, and was tireless in his efforts to improve life in "The Great Society." She may have been considered an enabler in tolerating her husband's often outrageous behavior, but what comes through in this biography is a "lady" in every sense of the word -- gracious, genuine, intelligent, loyal, steady, kind and considerate. When Sam Rayburn, former Speaker of the House and mentor of the young LBJ, told him, "The best decision you ever made was marrying Bird," Johnson responded, "There's not a day that goes by that I don't think of that." He knew her worth and the depth of her unconditional love, and it has been said that without Lady Bird there would never have been an LBJ. After reading this book, you are likely to agree.

$2.00 A DAY:
LIVING ON ALMOST NOTHING IN AMERICA

by
H. Luke Shaefer

In 1996 the 60 year-old welfare system that gave cash to poverty-stricken families with dependent children was abolished. Instead a new welfare program called "Temporary Assistance for Needy Families" replaced it. The results of this change is the subject of this book, *$2.00 a Day*. The author focuses on the four most destitute areas in the USA: the Mississippi Delta, the Appalachian region, and Chicago and Cleveland, the latter ranked #1 on "Forbes" list of "America's most miserable cities." Here many people live in inhabitable mobile homes in decrepit trailer parks; cheap, run-down apartments -- some without running water, heat, or electricity; homeless shelters; or dilapidated houses in dangerous and violent slum areas where families double up with three and four generations of parents, grandparents, children, and assorted uncles, aunts, and cousins living together in one very cramped dwelling. While the cost of housing has risen, wages have stagnated and jobs for the unskilled are scarce. In one instance, the author found twenty two family members living together on the income of one member. In another a family exists on Ramen noodles for two weeks of each month since the food allowance (SNAP given them by the government does not last the entire month. Poor nutrition and the toxic stress these families endure lead to physical and mental illnesses that in the end kill. Moreover, studies indicate that those without housing who depend on family and friends expose their kids to the risk of sexual, emotional, and physical abuse. Those with the largest number of caretakers are the most likely victims. These destitute and desperate people devise strategies to survive. One common way is selling their blood. In one family of four, the mother's donation of plasma for $30 a pint is the bedrock of their finances. In Tennessee, unlike other states, she is allowed to do this many times a month at the expense of her own health. Another strategy is seeking help from private charities, such as the Salvation Army, Goodwill, and Catholic Charity. In addition, these poor take advantage of public spaces like libraries -- not only for warmth, but also for use of the computer for job searches. They also often rely on soup kitchens, food pantries, and homeless shelters. However, there is a limit of two or three months stay in these shelters, so many find themselves lugging all they own in the world from one shelter to another. They must do this on foot since they have no transportation, not even money for bus fare.

Those who are able find low-paying work babysitting and clean-ing homes or find it necessary to resort to fencing stolen goods, selling drugs, or exchanging sex for necessities. One woman granted sexual favors to a man she knew well in return for having him pay her cell phone charges as well as the fee for a storage unit to house her few, but treasured belongings. Sometimes they trade SNAP (food allowance for cash in order to purchase needed under-wear and socks. One man relied on "scrapping," collecting aluminum cans to be recycled for cash, and sometimes found a discarded air-conditioner which would bring him $10-20 for its aluminum and copper content. But this type of scavenging takes long hours for very little profit. Another problem is staying clean, since detergent and laundromats require cash, which they don't have. Worse than this constant uncertainty and lack of stability day after day are the health hazards they face. One woman raising her family in the Sunshine County of the Mississippi Delta lives in an ancient sharecropper shack adjacent to fields with crops that are dusted with pesticides that also shower her home. Common to this area is a unique local upper respiratory ailment characterized by wheezing, nausea, and chronic congestion. Here health care ranks as the worst in the nation. Some counties don't even have an ambulance to get someone to the hospital, so the patient must be driven to the county line to meet an ambulance from another county; but these rural people do not own cars and are not on any transportation line. Even if buses were available, they have no money for the fare. Lack of transportation is also an impediment to finding employment in the larger cities. If one willing to work fills out an application and is called for an interview, first he/she needs to obtain costly appropriate clothing and then needs to traverse many miles to reach the destination, often arriving late, totally disheveled, and covered in perspiration from the trek -- not a very fortuitous appearance for a job-seeker. There are just so many obstacles they must surmount. "The work of survival at the very bottom of America's economic ladder is hard." This is indeed an understatement by the author. This population of Americans live in conditions equivalent to the poorest of the poor in Haiti or Zimbabwe. They don't even exist on government surveys because they have no permanent address; like nomads they move from place to place. As a result, it is difficult to identify how many there are.

The author predicts that the situation will become worse because technology is replacing the manual jobs formerly available to these uneducated, unskilled individuals. He does have some suggestions for improving their lot: increase in job training; increase in the minimum wage (which I believe has recently occurred; tutoring and after-school programs; safe and stimulating day care centers; funding for public libraries, pools and recreation centers; treatment centers for the chemically addicted; more shelters for the homeless; more affordable low-income housing; provision of full-time (not part-time employment; provision of predictable weekly work schedules; additional government rental subsidy vouchers; the installation of a "family crisis account" for working families to access when in dire need, and a finite number of times over a given period to apply for it. The "Temporary Assistance for Needy Families (TANF" which is now in existence is not working. This is a block grant given by the federal government to the states for the purpose of assisting those most in need with cash; but often it is siphoned off to pay for other expenses the state, in its strained budget, determines to be a priority.

I found this book both disturbing and enlightening because the author acquainted the reader with REAL people: their names, their history, their life stories and experiences, their hopes and dreams that we know will never be realized. THEY relate THEIR stories in graphic and heart-rending detail; and what tragic stories they are. These are people who never had a chance from the moment they were born, who have struggled every day of their lives just to survive, without the very basic necessities we take for granted. This book made them REAL to me.

Moreover, it impressed upon me and made me realize that it is next to impossible to procure the means for a decent life without ever having any cash -- NONE whatsoever. For most of us, even those who often don't have enough to easily make ends meet, it is unimaginable; but it is REALITY for these downtrodden poor.

CITIZENS OF LONDON:
THE AMERICANS WHO STOOD WITH BRITAIN
IN ITS DARKEST FINEST HOUR

by

Lynne Olson

Extremely well-researched, enlightening, and informative, *Citizens of London* is both history and biography about three men most instrumental in eliciting Pres. Franklin Delano Roosevelt's and America's support of Great Britain in the fight against Nazi Germany during WWII. One was the idealistic and altruistic John Gilbert Winant who replaced the disliked appeaser Joseph Kennedy as ambassador to The Court of St. James and became one of the most beloved saviors of the Brits. Another was Edward R. Murrow whose eloquent and visually descriptive radio broadcasts from Berlin, as well as war-torn London, stirred the hearts and minds of his listeners. It was said that Morrow's voice over the airwaves was "the only light in a world of darkness, bringing hope to those in despair," particularly those trapped by Nazi occupation where even owning a radio was punishable by death. In addition, was Averill Harriman, the aggressive, ambitious American entrepreneur who was appointed to oversee the flow of American aid to Europe under the Lend Lease Program. All three believed that US support was the only way to save England from defeat and worked tirelessly to that end. This is the totally engrossing story of those efforts amid political dissension and personality conflicts of powerful temperamental egotists like FDR and Winston Churchill, as well as adamant isolationists at home. Each was envious of the other: FDR of Churchill's genius; Churchill of FDR's power. This fascinating and mesmerizing tale reads like a novel with romance, glamour, danger, intrigue, wartime adventure, and larger-than-life personalities. In fact, that is one of Olson's finest abilities as an author -- the skillful revelation of the contradictory traits demonstrated by the genius statesman Churchill and others like Winant, who although disorganized and

171

scatter- brained, was probably the greatest asset to England in its fight-to-the death against Germany. Not only is this a story of political alliances but also of romantic relationships -- that of Winant with one of the Churchill daughters Sarah, in addition to the love affairs of both Harriman and Murrow with Pamela Churchill, daughter-in-law of the Prime Minister, ironic since Pamela's husband Randolph was assigned to direct Harriman in Algiers on a fact-finding mission on behalf of Winston. Truth is often stranger than fiction and that is the case in *Citizens in London.* Also of interest is the Brits' affection and adoration of the brash and handsome American fliers whose sometimes loud and boisterous behavior was dismissed as exuberance and tolerated because they were risking their lives daily in England's defense. These pilots brought hope and life to a weary and bomb-torn city. Other noteworthy characters on whom Olson focuses are the complex and unpretentious Dwight D. Eisenhower who despised the stiff upper-class world of the elite and their social scene. On the other hand, was Churchill who had absolutely no awareness of how the common people lived -- had never even been on a bus -- and favored the "good life." Nevertheless, it was their combined indefatigable energy, combativeness, courage, and dogged resolution that saved the country. Also significant was the vying for position and bickering concerning the management of postwar Europe once the mission was accomplished.

Believe it or not, there was NO plan which is why Stalin was easily able to dictate the terms regarding Poland and the remainder of Eastern-Europe. By that time both FDR and Churchill were battle-weary and very ill; Roosevelt died just a few weeks after the Potsdam Conference.

In this book the author Olson not only presents history in a very readable way but delves into the psychology of its main participants. Why did Morrow repeatedly put himself in life-threatening situations, accompanying pilots on twenty-four bombing raids into Germany? How did Gen. Eisenhower exude confidence and calm when, in fact, he was an emotional mess in the weeks prior to D-DAY, suffering from insomnia, headaches, stomach-pain, and skyrocketing blood pressure? Why did Winant take his own life after the war? Why did Harry Truman, President after FDR, immediately stop food aid to postwar England when it was bankrupt and people were homeless and starving?

Why was the heroic and highly revered Churchill voted out of office following the war? These are the many questions which Olson so thoroughly answers through her careful and perceptive analysis of these figures and events. This is one OUTSTANDING book whose title comes from an emotional final broadcast in 1940 by Eric Sevareid, then a 27 year-old correspondent leaving London: "When this is over, in the years to come, men will speak of the war and say, 'I was a soldier,' 'I was a sailor,' or 'I was a pilot.' Others will say with equal pride, 'I was a citizen of London.' "There is poetic prose as well when he compares Paris days before its fall to the Germans as "dying like a beautiful woman, in a coma, without struggle.... while London alone behaves with pride, and battered but stubborn dignity." The men in this book saved the civilized world and for that reason alone this book is a suitable tribute to them, highly worth reading.

BEHIND THE BEAUTIFUL FOREVERS
LIFE, DEATH, AND HOPE IN A MUMBAI UNDERCITY

by
Kate Boo

DESPAIR. HOPELESSNESS. INJUSTICE. CORRUPTION. HUNGER. DIRE POVERTY. ILLITERACY. LACK OF OPPORTUNITY. OPPRESSION. DEPRIVATION. PHYSICAL AND EMOTIONAL ABUSE. ILLNESS. FILTH. LACK OF HUMAN RIGHTS. ABSENCE OF DECENCY. ILLITERACY. SUPERSTITION. IGNORANCE. DYSFUNC-TIONAL GOVERNMENT. All describe the hell-hole of existence that is Annawadi, the squatter slum settlement outside the International Airport in Mumbai, India. Here 3,000 people are tightly packed into and atop 335 ram-shackle huts next to a sewage lake, which gives rise to malaria and dengue fever. The walls of the huts are green and black with mold; foot fungus is ram-pant. Contents of the public toilet (a hole in the ground) overflows into the main road. A 500 bed hospital lacking the most basic medical necessities -- water, bandages, burn balm -- cannot support the one million in the surround-ing vicinity that depend upon it. Patients lie on urine soaked mattresses, hooked to IV bags with used syringes because to use a new one on every pa-tient would be wasteful. Here live (if one can call it "living") Asha, Manju, Ab-dul, Sunil, Kalu who must depend on their wits and luck to survive in this abys-mal place, over ridden with pigs, rats, lice, and all other types of vermin.

Abdul's family of twelve squeeze together in one room atop each other, where during sleep one child's foot often lies in another's mouth; and, due to lack of floor space, some cannot stretch out but rather doze upright against a wall. Since the age of six he has been trafficking in rich people's gar-bage which he can obtain at the dumpsters behind the wall at the airport. Plas-tics, in particular, can be hauled to recycling stations for small payment, so he spends all day sifting through empty water and whisky bottles, mildewed newspapers, used tampon applicators, yellowed Q-tips, etc. He chews the plastic, first, to determine its grade, as well as inhaling it to determine its polyurethane content. His father's lungs have become blackened from such work. Some of these scavengers are found dead by the roadside, often the victims of gangs who profit from the same type of work and dislike competition. Also along this airport road lie emaciated junkies or cripples hit by cars speeding by. No one stops and police cannot be bothered to properly investigate such insignificant beings. Scavenging is neither easy nor safe; scrapes from diving into dumpsters become infected, skin breaks, and maggots settle in, often leading to gangrene. For all this, sometimes the meager take is thirty three cents a day. Incredibly, here and there can be found a budding scholar who studies long into the night hours in hopes of going to college or at least obtaining a job as a doorman at one of the elegant hotels, or better yet at an internet call center if one can learn English. Unfortunately, much about the schools is fraudulent since sixty percent of teachers never completed college and many pay large sums under-the-table to obtain their positions. Even if they did finish college, instruction is rote memorization devoid of any intellectual analysis or dissection. The main reason some students attend school is for the free lunch; and school consists of play, rest, and recess rather than true learning. Most kids need to be out contributing to the support of their families, with no time to attend school. American altruists who want to contribute, such as the World Vision Charity, send goods which never arrive to their intended recipients, but instead fall into the hands of slum lords who sell the items for their own profit. Corruption is widespread everywhere -- in government, police, even among doctors, who don't earn enough to support their own families. Innocent people can be unjustly accused of a crime, arrested, tortured, and beaten; but charges can be dropped for the required bribe. Courtrooms are places of pandemonium where hallways become encampments where family members, eat, pray, and doze against greasy tiled walls. Plastic bottles and cans litter the floor. In the courtroom, horns from cars and trains, as well as throttling engines, make it difficult to hear testimony which is often inaccurately interpreted since the witnesses often speak in an unfamiliar dialect. The trials continue for months, many different trials held simultaneously, with fifteen to thirty minutes devoted to each one before the judge rapidly moves on to the next.

Hence, sometimes the judge with whom the trial began is not the same judge with whom it ends, and the latter has inaccurate records of the preceding testimony. It is common for witnesses, over such long periods of time, to forget or even change their testimony due to bribery. Such unfair experiences, in a world over which these Indians feel they have no control, leads to hopelessness and despondency, and many take their own lives. The most common method is consuming rat poison or setting oneself on fire. These are real people the author interviewed or relatives of these people. The reader cannot help but care about them, grieve for them, feel empathy for their sad lot. This is a heart-rending and sobering book, certainly not for the faint-hearted; but so worth the reader's time for its enlightening and provocative information about a forgotten portion of one of the 21st century's most important world cities.

THE BRIDGE LADIES

by

Betsy Lerner

A "Bridge-Lady" myself, I was drawn to this book which is quite unique in that the author employs the game of bridge for a number of purposes: first, to learn the basics of playing; secondly, to understand the female attitudes and mores of what has been called "The Greatest Generation"; and most importantly, to connect with her mother with whom she has always had an uneasy relationship. Although she is intent on learning the conventions of the game -- bidding, trumping, taking tricks, and ruffing -- her main focus is on the four-some of which her mother is a player. Lerner observes that during games they never discuss "heavy" or serious issues -- personal or otherwise; that each one prides herself on setting a beautiful table for lunch first (to the author an anachronism from the past and that once the game begins, all conversation ceases. Gradually she befriends each of her mother's group and discovers that beneath their well-groomed, perfectly coiffed, composed personas are real people who may have chosen the traditional role of wife and mother, but who also felt and experienced life as keenly and acutely as their younger counterparts. They were not like those in the author's age group who rebelled, "dropping out of college, dropping acid, dropping out of life." They toed the line, followed rules, and often sacrificed their personal dreams and ambitions for what their parents and society expected of them. Nor did they visit analysts with whom to share their personal problems, disappointments, and tragedies; not that they didn't experience these issues. They simply chose to deal with them in a less vocal, more reticent, more contained manner. As one example, this new proximity to her mother allows mother and daughter to finally discuss a family secret which has always remained shrouded in mystery -- the death of Betsy's 6 year-old sister. Betsy has no memory of this sibling, but at the time keenly sensed her mother's withdrawal from the family. As Betsy probes

179

deeper, her mother reluctantly finally acknowledges that painful loss as well as her struggle with post-partum depression following Betsy's birth. In unburdening herself of her own vulnerabilities and shortcomings, the mother is better able to connect emotionally with the daughter who always felt she could never measure up to her mother's obsolete standards. By spending time together learning the card game, both are able to "bridge" the gap which has separated them for so long. In regard to the other members of the group, they too become less resistant, opening up sufficiently to share their memories and feelings about past choices -- allowing themselves to be seen "naked" to some degree. The author speculates that this older generation must think their children's lives look like "a massive oil spill off the Carolina's."

There are elements of humor as well. For example, as beginner Betsy struggles to master the etiquette of the game -- keeping track of who shuffles, who deals, who cuts -- her cognitive skills are so stressed that she quips she was "more relaxed the first time she lost her virginity." She also speculates that perhaps she needs "Bridge-Special Education" or a chair marked with a handicapped sign.

For those who love bridge -- and even for those who don't play -- this is a frank and provocative memoir of the new bond that develops between a mother and daughter after years of hurts, slights, and misunderstandings. It is an uplifting, life-affirming story about repairing a conflict-ridden relationship all too common among mothers and their daughters. Moreover, you might be inclined to take up this challenging game as medical evidence indicates that it helps to delay dementia and has social benefits that prolong life.

TWO SOULS INDIVISIBLE:
THE FRIENDSHIP THAT SAVED TWO POWS IN VIETNAM

by

James S. Hirsch

Two Souls Indivisible is the remarkable and harrowing story of two POWs, Porter Halyburton, a white gentlemanly Navy lieutenant flier -- college graduate, poet, and scholar, -- and Fred Cherry, a black major in the US Air Force, considered "one of their best combat pilots." Both were shot down by enemy fire over Vietnam and confined and tortured for more than seven years. The abuse by their captors was brutal, and Cherry was on the brink of death more than once. After four years of solitary confinement in extremely cramped dark cells of freezing concrete floors overrun by web-footed gray rats, scorpions, and ants, and existing on a daily diet of moldy bread and watery soup containing cockroaches, Halyburton's resolve to live was waning. Four weeks before he left for military service, his wife Marty had given birth to an infant daughter Dabny for whom he yearned to be reunited someday; but he had begun to lose hope that he would ever see them again. At the very nadir of his existence, Halyburton was moved to a different cell where a very seriously injured, feverish Cherry, his shoulder wrenched from its socket, the entire arm dangling limp about to fall off, was hovering between life and death. Cherry had come from Room Eighteen which had soundproofed walls to deaden the screams of the prisoners as they were interrogated and tortured. From the ceiling was suspended a giant hook on which the prisoners were strung up with ropes tied around their arms, the cord oiled to make the pain more intense. The guard's order to Halyburton: "You must take care of Cherry." And so began one of the most remarkable encounters in military history. Each was wary of the other. Halyburton, a product of the South, had been raised to believe that blacks were intellectually inferior, had never known a black pilot, wasn't even sure that they had the depth perception necessary for flying. In addition, he had never known a black who outranked him. Similarly, Cherry distrusted this young white Navy lieutenant. Despite intense beatings, he had refused to give up any information, and so he assumed that Halyburton was a spook, whose Southern accent was part of a plot to trick him into giving information. Indeed, part of the enemy's cunning was to increase this Southern boy's discomfit by giving him a negro cellmate since they were very aware of the racial tension in the US. For his part, Cherry had never been treated respectfully by whites, either in his youth or later in the military. Blacks had been segregated because it was the general belief that they were unfit to lead. Cherry was the exception and his performances dazzled his commanders. But this bias increased his pressure to perform, and was also the reason he refused to cooperate with the Vietnamese who demanded he condemn his government in statements. Even after the "fan belt treatment" -- being hit was bamboo or rubber strips, raising welts upon his back, -- he would not give in. By then he and Porter had been separated. For ninety three days, they put Cherry in leg irons and chained him to his bed board, his arms tied behind him despite the fact that one had been torn from its socket and was dangling limply. Confined like this, Cherry still defied his captors, knocking his head against the cement wall so that the bumps resembled the code Halyburton had taught him when they were together. Even in unimaginable agony, he was transmitting information about enemy tactics. in this way, Cherry's resilience and resourcefulness made him a legend among POWs. Halyburton was simultaneously suffering his own torture elsewhere. With his arms behind his back, a pair of "rachet cuffs" on his wrists were slid down to his forearms, the cuffs chain wrapped around the outside exerting intense pressure on his forearms. Then draping a rope around his neck, they tied his neck to his leg irons. Pulling the rope forced him to bend forward, causing great stress on his body and tightening the cuffs around his forearms. These were only two of the sadistic forms of torture endured by these brave individuals. But the most awe-inspiring portion of the book is how these two men were victorious in their exercise of humanity over inhumanity. During their imprisonment together, each man gave the other the incentive to resist and endure. In Cherry's most weakened state – eighty five pounds, frail, wasted, unable to stand -- his friend lifted him over a bucket pulled to the side of the bed to defecate; washed him daily with a dirty rag; treated as best he could the constantly puss-oozing shoulder and bloody bedsores; screamed and demanded medical care for Cherry, citing the rules of the Geneva Convention regarding treatment of war prisoners, demanding blood transfusions and antibiotic intravenous; for hours all through the night lifting and releasing a too-tight cast every time Cherry inhaled because it was suffocating him. On another occasion Cherry had been drenched in gasoline, poured into the neck portion of the cast to counteract the putrid odor of his decaying flesh beneath it. Much later, when allowed a rare shower, Porter scrubbed and scrubbed with his soapy hands and nails to get the vermin off Fred's body and out of his hair. It always impressed Cherry that such a thing would be unthinkable in America, but how the POW camp had made this possible. Again and again Halyburton did all he could to relieve and assuage his partner's suffering. Except for one occasion, he always offered Cherry first their meager portion of food. "He kept me alive," declared Cherry; "It was a privilege," asserted Halyburton.

I was the one privileged to see and hear these extraordinary, but humble men sit on a stage at the Naval War College in Newport, Rhode Island. Their respect and love for each other was palpable even in a room of many. Halyburton said that "their friendship renewed his spirits and motivated him to find meaning in his captivity ... the task of caring for him gave a definite purpose to my immediate existence." It is impossible for me to try to explain the honor I felt to be in their presence, as true a hero as any I had ever read about in the history books. I was even more impressed when Halyburton's wife Marty arranged for him to redesign my rock garden in Bristol, Rhode Island where we were neighbors. She had really never given up, even when told he was dead, even after his funeral and memorial service. They went on to have two more children when he returned, settling in my Bristol neighborhood, and teaching at The Naval War College mentioned above. I cannot say I personally knew Porter, but that day watching him dig and plant in my garden, I had to remind myself that this tall, quiet, dignified, patient, and deeply religious man had endured so much hardship and suffering and had survived. Outside my window worked a man who reflected our country's highest ideals of sacrifice and honor, and I felt a limitless gratitude to him and his comrades. Halyburton once asserted that he was "in awe of Cherry and had learned to love him' and that Cherry was "his superior in rank and reality." In my humble opinion, both were superhuman in every way -- character, integrity, honor, humanity. I saw them cry as they embraced each other on that stage and I was deeply moved. In the horrendous atmosphere of a prison camp, together they had created "a more perfect America" than Cherry had ever found in America itself.

GREAT BOOKS

GREAT BOOKS NOT TO BE MISSED

The Glass Castle (Jeannette Walls)

This is a touching memoir of a child raised in an extremely dysfunctional family who not only survives intact but becomes highly successful as well. To mention just a few of her mishaps with her irresponsible parents: she falls out of a speeding car with her drunken father at the wheel and no one notices she is gone for many miles; her father steals the money she and her brother have been saving from odd jobs for many months -- their intention was to use it to escape this unsettled life where the family must repeatedly run away under cover of darkness to avoid eviction for non-payment of rent. Often they sleep in an open field under the stars where in her early childhood she believed her adored father's promises that he would build her "a glass castle" in the sky where they would all live happily together. This is human drama at its best -- personal and deeply experienced.

Sarah's Key (Tatiana deRosnay)

One of the most heart-wrenching stories I have ever read about a young Jewish girl taken by the Nazis during the Holocaust, who, in order to hide and save her younger brother, locks him in a cupboard. Much of the book is devoted to her determined efforts to retrieve him, as well as a separate story about the new residents of the apartment in which she was forced to leave him. A compelling story, deeply moving, set amid the horrors of war.

One True Thing (Anna Quindlen)

Lest I dwell on heartbreaking stories, this one is deeply moving and will not only grip and hold your attention but also remain with you long after you've finished the book. The main character (played by Meryl Streep in the movie version becomes terminally ill; and her husband, a college professor, expects their career-oriented daughter to return home from her newspaper job to care for her mother. Although the author insists that this story is not autobiographical, there are enough similarities between the novel and Quindlen's real life, to make one wonder. The very best part of the book is the relationship and understanding that develops between mother and daughter. An ambitious girl, the daughter has always adored her charismatic father (as do some of his female students as well, and has dismissed the mother as merely a traditional wife and homemaker without any particular talents or accomplishments -- who has wasted her life catering to her family and making a comfortable home. Only in those last months together does she see the true dynamics of her family and realize that for all these years, her perception of her mother has been incorrect. There are deeply wrought key moments throughout the story that foreshadow the reality that has escaped the daughter all these years; and with a pang of awareness she realizes finally that it is her mother who is the strong, supportive core of this family unit and has held all of them together. The mystery that is resolved in the final chapters is a shocking surprise to the reader and a tribute to the mother's love to protect them all.

Seabiscuit: An American Legend (Laura Hillenbrand)

A truly captivating and engrossing tale of a marvelous racehorse who was the subject of most newspaper columns between 1936 - 1940.

Seabiscuit, crooked and undersized, underestimated by all, became a cultural icon in the latter half of the Depression -- not surprising, since there were so many underdogs, both animal and human, who were inspired by his indefatigable spirit and will. This is also the story of his trainer, Tom Smith, a taciturn cowboy from the vanishing Western frontier and his jockey, Red Pollard. The book is set in the world of horse stables, famous race locations like Santa Anita, the Kentucky Derby, Belmont Park, Pimlico (Maryland. etc. Fast-paced and dramatic, Hillenbrand's writing style superbly captures the excitement and hysteria of these contests so well that the reader can almost see and hear the crowds of spectators going wild as these extraordinary animals and their skilled riders streak by lap after lap. The book is very well-researched so that the author is able to vividly recreate an unforgettable time in horse- racing history. It will hold your attention from the start to the "finish" line.

The Memory Keeper's Daughter (Kim Edwards)

During a blizzard, a doctor is forced to deliver his own twins, in his office with only the assistance of his nurse. One child is perfect; the other a Down Syndrome baby. Without the knowledge of his anesthetized wife, he instructs the nurse to take the second to an institution. This decision will affect all of their lives, in ways he could never have foreseen, drawing the reader completely into the character's mind. This is a story of long-held secrets and the damage they wreak on a marital relationship, as well as the guilt, regret, and sense of loss that ensues as a result.

Snow Falling on Cedars (David Guterson)

A beautifully written tale of young love between an American boy and a Japanese girl who are eventually separated due to her family's internment of Japanese in California following the bombing of Pearl Harbor. The plot is intricate and will develop into the investigation of the mysterious death of one of the characters and an ensuing court trial. Not only is the story suspenseful, but also enlightening regarding the bigotry and mass hysteria that evolved as a result of this historic attack. It is a combination of romance and mystery, set against an historical background.

When the Emperor Was Divine (Julie Otsuka)

Like the novel above, this one also focuses on this sad chapter in our nation's history, the internment of Japanese-Americans following the attack on Pearl Harbor. This poignant tale is told through the viewpoints of a young brother and sister whose father is arrested and taken to a camp in the middle of the night. Later they and their mother will also be relocated to a different camp. During their three and a half years of confinement, they suffer untold hardship: concern for the disappearance of their father; housing in freezing make-shift barracks improvised from horse stables; constant hunger from meagerly rationed food; illness resulting from the constant wind and dust-storms of the Utah desert where they are sequestered; anxiety, depression, despair, and hopelessness. The author keenly evokes the reader's sympathy for these innocent children, who even after the war, are shunned, isolated, and emotionally damaged forever. It is a deeply moving tale of human drama.

OTHER OUTSTANDING READS

OTHER OUTSTANDING READS

The Gold Coast (Nelson DeMille)

The General's Daughter (Nelson DeMille)

The Reader (Bernard Schlink)

Cold Mountain (Charles Frazier)

Hotel on the Corner of Bitter and Sweet (Jamie Ford)

Defending Jacob (William Landay)

The Help (Katherine Stockett)

Unbroken (Laura Hillenbrand)

Atonement (Ian McEwan)

Suite Francaise (Irène Némirovsky)

The Storyteller (Jodi Picoult)

Too Rich (biography of Doris Duke by Pony Duke)

The Immortal Cells of Henrietta Lacks (Rebecca Skloot)

Killing Lincoln (Bill O'Reilly)

Team of Rivals (Doris Kearns Goodwin)

The Kite Runner (Khaled Hosseini)

The Presidents' Club (Gibbs & Duffy)

Too Close to the Sun (Curtis Roosevelt)

In the Garden of Beasts (Erik Larson)

Hidden Power: Presidential Marriages That Shaped Our Recent History (Kate Morton)

Plainsong (Kent Haruf)

This Boy's Life (Tobias Wolf)

A Woman in Berlin (Anonymous)

The Book Thief (Markus Zusak)

It's All Over but the Shoutin' (Rick Bragg)

American Heiress (Daisy Goodwin)

Loving Frank (Nancy Horan)

Angela's Ashes (Frank McCourt)

The Postmistress (Sarah Blake)

Age of Innocence (Edith Wharton)

The Invisible Wall (Harry Bernstein)

Made in the USA
San Bernardino, CA
15 January 2017